*The* **African-American**
*child's*
**Heritage COOKBOOK**

# VANESSA ROBERTS PARHAM

*Sandcastle Publishing*

# The African-American Child's Heritage Cookbook

Copyright © 1993 by Vanessa Roberts Parham
Book Interior and Cover Design, R. Rolle-Whatley

This publication is designed to provide accurate and authoritative information in regard to the subject covered. Although the author has tested all recipies, both author and publisher assume no responsibility for errors, inaccuracies, omissions or any other inconsistency herein. Any slights against people or organizations are unintentional.

## Publisher's Cataloging in Publication
(Prepared by Quality Books Inc.)

Parham, Vanessa Roberts, 1950-
    The African-American child's heritage cookbook / Vanessa Roberts Parham.
    p. cm.
    Includes glossary and index.
    SUMMARY: A collection of recipes for children instructing them in the traditions of African-American cooking. Includes brief history of African-American cooking.
    Pre-assigned LCCN: 92-60006.
    ISBN 0-9627756-2-2

    1. Cookbooks--Ethnic, international. 2. Afro-American cookery--Juvenile literature. I. Title.

TX715.2.A57P37 1992            641.592'96073
                            QBI92-20053

Printed in the United States of America

6 5 4 3 2 1

Cover Photograph by Paul Downs

For additional copies, use the order form at the back of the book or write to:
SANDCASTLE PUBLISHING, Customer Inquiries,
P.O. Box 3070, South Pasadena, California 91031-6070

# Dedication

This book is for people of all colors, and especially those of African-American descent. We are indebted to the generations before us who combined their African culinary techniques with Native American, Spanish, French, and Caribbean cookery to create a taste that lives today.

It is my most sincere hope that this book will bring grandmothers and their daughters, sons and grand-children into the kitchen to try new dishes and rediscover old favorites.

Please use these recipes and teach our future generations just how sweet it was and how sweet it can be.

# Acknowledgements

For their inspiration and steadfast encouragement during all the years I worked on this cookbook, my love and deepest thanks are extended. . .

To my parents, the late James and Arnesia Roberts,

To my husband, Douglas R. Parham,

To my son, Douglas R. Parham, II (Robbie)

To my sister, Janice Hamilton, and the rest of my family, auntie and cousins in Washington, VA,

To my co-workers at Benjamin Banneker School in L.A., especially Donna Adams, Liz McClellan and Lula Wilson,

To Kenneth Green for the fabulous sketches,

And to my many friends in NY, NJ, AL, GA, DC and Los Angeles, California.

To my grandmother, La Jonne Pope, who is 82 and still cooking everyday, you're wonderful!

I would also like to thank Jennie Kuroyama, Sarah Lamar, Taylor Redd, Jr, and Wayne Mason for their contributions. Without their help, completion of this book would not have been possible.

Lastly, my sincere thanks go out to my editors at Sandcastle Publishing, Renee Rolle-Whatley and Gary Whatley for believing in my book and spending countless hours bringing it all together.

# Contents

## The Beginning:
*The Motherland*

## The Beginning:
*In the United States, 1619*

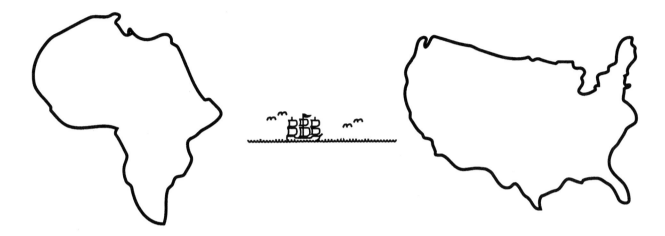

West African cooking is a composite of cooking skills used by different nations with various levels of education, social development, and degrees of wealth. In every African nation, cooking was one of the most important skills which young girls had to master. Most African men were farmers, cattle raisers and fishermen. Planting, sowing and harvesting crops were women's work in most of West Africa. One traditional dish called *fufu* was made of pounded yams and served with soup, stew, roasted meat and different sauces. Cooking was done over open pits. Africans were advanced in roasting, frying, stewing, boiling and steaming their foods. Native foods are yams, okra, watermelon, cassava, groundnuts, black-eyed peas and rice.

The first group of Africans in America landed at Jamestown, Virginia in August, 1619, as indentured servants. Southern plantations consisted of many tribal nations which made up the slave population in southern America. Verbal exchanges of recipes led to the development of an international African cooking style in America. The slaves cooked pork (fatback), yams, sweet potatoes, corn, hominy, hoecakes, ashcakes, cabbage, collards and cowpeas. Cooking was done on an open fireplace with large swing blackpots and big skillets.

# HISTORY OF AFRICAN-AMERICAN COOKING

## American Revolution:
*Colonial Period, 1776*

## Emancipation:
*Civil War Period, 1865*

*by Kenneth Green*

Between 1773 and 1785 thousands of Africans were brought ashore in Virginia, the Carolinas (Sea Island) and Georgia. Slaves were cooks, gardeners and servants. They dominated the colonial kitchens and worked on the plantations as field hands. At the Big House such foods as spoonbread, crab cakes, corn pones, corn pudding, greens and succotash were cooked on an open pit or fireplace. On the plantation, breakfast was an important and early meal. Hoecake and molasses were eaten as the slaves worked from sunup to sundown.

African-Americans were hired as cooks for both the northern and the southern armies. African-Americans did most of the cooking throughout the south. Slaves invented their own recipes and made the best of hard times with their scarce supplies. Creole and Cajun cooking developed during this time. Examples: jambalaya, bread pudding, dirty rice, gumbo and red beans and rice. Cooking was done on a great big old fireplace with swing pots and skillets with legs.

## <u>Westward The Exodus:</u>
*Moving West, 1870-1890*

*by Kenneth Green*

The end of the Civil War and Emancipation saw many African-Americans move west to Kansas, Nebraska, Oklahoma and Texas. They became cowboys and cooks on the cattle drives. Many were pioneers, and as farmers they survived off the land, adapting their cooking habits and forming new ones when necessary. It was a great challenge to create good food with primitive tools and limited ingredients. These foods were biscuits, barbequed meat, stew and baked beans.

## <u>The Great Migration:</u>
*1900-1945*

A large number of African-Americans continue to contribute to America's foodways as cooks in private homes, shops, restaurants, hotels, schools and colleges. Many moved to major cities for work in such places as Chicago, New York, Ohio, Detroit and Pennsylvania. Black cooks, chefs and waiters established fine dining and elegant service in the Pullman cars of the old railroads and on the steamboats. Many African-Americans started small businesses such as barbecue and soul food joints and fish markets throughout the United States. These eateries specialized in fried fish, homemade rolls, potato salad, turkey and dressing, fried pork chops, rice and gravy and southern fried chicken, which is legendary throughout the United States. Cooking was done on woodburning and gas stoves.

### Civil Rights Movement:
*1965-Present*

by Kenneth Green

In the early 60's and 70's, soul food, the traditional food of African-Americans, was very popular. These foods were candied yams, okra, fried chicken, cornbread, pigs feet, chitlin's, collard greens with ham hocks and black-eyed peas. But in the 80's and now the 90's, soul food preparation methods have changed. African-Americans today are increasingly health conscious. By avoiding foods with high levels of fat and cholesterol, and increasing their intake of fruit, vegetables and fiber, many African-Americans have been able to improve their health and reduce their risk of high blood pressure, heart disease and cancer.

African-Americans are still in the kitchen cooking, but now are owners and managers of restaurants. McDonald's, Burger King, Church's Chicken and Kentucky Fried Chicken are just a few of these eateries. African-American chefs and professional caterers in restaurants and big hotels can be found throughout the United States. Today cooking is done on electric, gas and microwave stoves.

January 1st

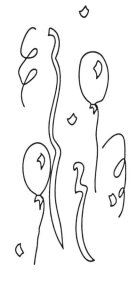

**New Year's Day** brings with it new hopes for the coming months.

Traditional foods on New Year's Day:

*Black-eyed Peas* - represent good luck or good fortune
*Rice* - represents prosperity
*Greens* - represent money
*Fish* - represents motivation and the desire to increase your wealth.

January 15th

**Dr. Martin Luther King Jr.'s Birthday**
In 1986, the first U.S. African-American national holiday was celebrated. "Soul Food" is traditional fare on this day.

February

**Black History Month**
Started by Dr. Carter Goodwin Woodson in 1926 as Negro History Week. February is the month to celebrate Black Heritage with "down-home" (Soul Food) cooking . This fare includes such dishes as Fried Chicken, Fried Fish, Collard Greens, Okra-Corn-Tomatoes, Sweet Potatoes and Cornbread.

African Flag symbology:
Red is for the blood of African People;
Black is for the face of African People;
Green is for hope and Africa.

February or March

**Mardi Gras** is French for *Fat Tuesday*, because it always falls on the Tuesday before Ash Wednesday. During Mardi Gras Creole food is served. Creole is a term used to identify a person of mixed French and Black or Spanish and Black ancestry from Louisiana. The French were the first settlers in New Orleans. They borrowed spices and seasonings from the Choctaw Indians; Africans came with herbs and vegetables; and the Spanish with peppers. When everything was mixed together Creole cooking was born. Some typical creole foods are Gumbo, Red Beans and Rice, Jambalaya, Dirty Rice and Bread Pudding.

June 19

**Juneteenth** started in Texas during the Civil War. News of the official Emancipation Proclamation Day, effective January 1, 1863, did not reach the slaves in Texas until June, 1865. Today people celebrate June 19th by having barbecues and picnics on "Juneteenth." Such foods as ribs, chicken, baked beans, potato salad, coleslaw and peach cobbler are served.

June, July or August

are months for **Family Reunions** where African-American families gather together to research their roots. Remembering who you are, where you came from and what you're made of is very important at these gatherings. Usually families and friends get together and have old-fashioned picnics with real "down home" foods—ribs, chicken, hot links, salads, fresh fruits in season and cobblers.

December 26-January 1

**Kwanzaa,** an African-American holiday to remember our ancestors, founded in 1966 by Dr. Maulana "Ron" Karenga. Usually foods of African and southern backgrounds such as Jollof Rice, Chicken in Groundnut Sauce, African Salad and Fried Plantains are served.

Sunday Dinner

**Traditional Family Dinners** are large family affairs. This is the time to eat and share favorite foods with friends and kin, a time for hospitality toward neighbors, and a time to inspire positive thoughts and strong family ties. Foods served are; Ham, Southern Fried Chicken, Potato Salad, String Beans with Potatoes, Pound Cake or Lemon Meringue Pie.

# KWANZAA
## (Kwahn-zah)

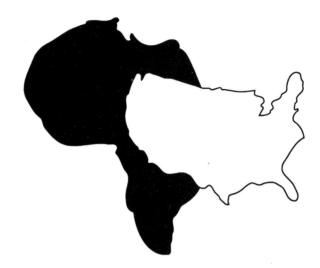

The Basics of Kwanzaa:

What is it? — An African-American holiday to remember our ancestors.

What does it mean? — Kwanzaa means "First Fruits".

When did it start? — Founded on December 26, 1966, by Dr. Maulana "Ron" Karenga.

How long does it last? — There are seven days of Kwanzaa. It begins on December 26 and ends on January 1st.

What are the Rules? — There are seven Principles or Rules for the seven days called *Nguzo Saba* (n-goo-zoh sah-ba).

# KWANZAA DAYS

Day 1   **UMOJA** (oo-moe-ja)
means UNITY
Togetherness in family, community, nation and race.

Day 2   **KUJICHAGULIA** (coo-gee-cha-goo-lee-ah)
means SELF-DETERMINATION
Thinking for yourself.

Day 3   **UJIMA** (oo-GEE-mah)
means COLLECTIVE WORK AND RESPONSIBILITY
Working together to help others.

Day 4   **UJAMAA** (oo-JAH-mah)
means COOPERATIVE ECONOMIES
Own businesses and jobs.

Day 5   **NIA** (nee-ah)
means PURPOSE
To build and develop our communities in order to be the
great people that we are.

Day 6   **KUUMBA** (coo-OOM-bah)
means CREATIVITY
To do as much as we can to make our communities beautiful.

Day 7   **IMANI** (ee-MAH-nee)
means FAITH
To believe in God, parents, teachers, leaders and the
goodness and victory of our struggle.

# 7 SYMBOLS OF KWANZAA

1. **MAZAO**
   **(Crops)**

Fruits and vegetables signify rewards from the work we do

2. **MKEKA**
   **(Place Mat)**

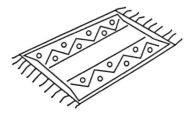

Straw Mat represents our foundation

3. **KINARA**
   **(Candleholder)**

This represents our family background (ancestors) and where we all come from (Africa)

4. **VIBUNZI**
   **(Ears of corn)**

Represents children

5. **ZAWADI**
   **(Gifts)**

Represent rewards for good work

6. **KIKOMBE CHA UMOJA**
   **(Unity Cup)**

Represents unity. Everyone drinks from the same cup

7. **MISUMMA SABA**
   **(The Seven Candles)**

This represents the Nguzo Saba— Seven Principles of Kwanzaa

African-American cooking techniques and recipes were influenced by Native American Indians all across the United States.

| Area | Indian Tribes & Confederations | Food |
|---|---|---|
| <u>Northeastern</u><br>New York-<br>Virginia | Iroquois<br>Powhatan | Fruit, fish & game, beans, corn, squash |
| <u>New England</u><br>Massachusetts | Narragansett<br>Penobscot | Lobster, oysters, clams, maple syrup, succotash, corn pudding, pumpkin pie, Indian pudding |
| <u>Southern</u><br>North Carolina<br>South Carolina<br>Florida<br>Louisiana | Cherokee<br>Creek<br>Seminole<br>Catawba | Beans, corn, squash |
| <u>Midwest</u><br>Plains | Cheyenne<br>Crow<br>Dakota | Jerky (dried meat or fish) |
| <u>Southwestern</u><br>Texas<br>Arizona<br>New Mexico | Hopi<br>Pueblo<br>Apache<br>Navajo | Chilies, melons, fry bread |

When Africans were first brought to America in 1620, they lived on farms. In many areas, local Indians taught them how to hunt and cook with native plants.

Indian cooking techniques were later introduced into southern society by African-American cooks. Dishes, such as Hominy Grits, Brunswick Stew, Sassafras and filé, used to thicken soups and stews (Creole Gumbo), are but a few examples.

Native American dishes found in African American Heritage Cooking:

|  |  |
| --- | --- |
| Corn Pudding | see page 187 |
| Brunswick Stew | see page 146 |
| Succotash | see page 83 |

| | |
|---|---|
| **BAKE** | To cook in an oven. |
| **BASTE** | To spoon sauce over whatever is cooking. |
| **BEAT** | To stir a mixture smooth with a spoon, or by using an egg beater, electric mixer or whisk. |
| **BLEND** | To mix two or more ingredients thoroughly. |
| **BOIL** | Heat liquid up enough to make bubbles appear. |
| **BROIL** | To cook directly under a flame or heating unit. |
| **BROWN** | Cook in a small amount of oil to give food some color. |
| **CHILL** | To put in refrigerator to get cold. |
| **CHOP** | To cut food into little pieces. |
| **COMBINE** | Mix together. |
| **CREAM** | Mix together till very smooth. |
| **CUBE** | Cut in squares. |
| **CUT-IN** | To use two forks, two knives or a pastry blender to combine solid shortening with dry ingredients until mixture resembles small peas. |

| | |
|---|---|
| **DICE** | Cut in little squares. |
| **DOT** | To cover surfaces with tiny pieces of butter or cheese. |
| **DISSOLVE** | To stir into a smooth solution. |
| **Drain** | Let water run off whatever you are making. |
| **DREDGE** | To coat with flour or sometime crumbs. |
| **DRIZZLE** | To pour gently from a spoon. |
| **FLOUR** | To coat a greased pan lightly by shaking flour over surface. |

| | |
|---|---|
| **FOLD** | To add an ingredient with gentle overlapping strokes. |
| **FRY** | To heat in oil until crispy in frying pan or skillet. |
| **GRATE** | To cut food into tiny pieces by rubbing it up and down on a grater. |
| **GREASE** | To rub a butter, margarine, vegetable oil spray or other shortening on the inside of a pan to prevent sticking. |
| **KNEAD** | To work dough with your hands by folding over, pressing and squeezing. |
| **MARINATE** | To let food stand in liquid that will add flavor or tenderize before cooking. |
| **MELT** | Heat until liquid. |

# COOKING TERMS

**MINCE**     To chop very fine.

**MIX**     Combine ingredients evenly.

**PAN-BROIL**     To cook in skillet on top of stove.

**PARBOIL**     To partially cook in boiling water.

**PANFRY**     Cook in small amount of oil in skillet.

**PARE**     Cut off outer skin as from an apple or potato.

**PEEL**     Pull off outer skin, as from an orange or banana.

**PINCH**     A little, little bit—just what can be pinched up with two fingers.

**PREHEAT**     To turn oven on and get it heated to the temperature called for in your recipe before you put what you are cooking in the oven.

**ROAST**     To cook meat in an oven.

**ROLL OUT**     Flatten and spread with a rolling pin.

**SAUTE**     To brown quickly in a small amount of butter or oil.

**SCALD**     Heating the milk until it's almost boiling. It's the right temperature when tiny bubbles appear around the edge of the milk and it starts to steam.

**SEPARATE AN EGG**     To break an egg in such a way that the yolk and white may be used separately.

**SHRED**     To tear or cut into long pieces by using a grater or food processor.

**SIFT**     Put ingredients in a sifter to make them very fine.

**SIMMER**     Cook in liquid almost to boiling but not hot enough to bubble.

**STIR**     Mix round and round with spoon.

**TOAST**     To brown food lightly.

**TOSS**     Mix lightly.

**WHIP**     Beat with hand beater, electric mixer or whisk to add air.

### BEFORE YOU BEGIN
1. Get permission to use the kitchen.
2. Wash your hands.
3. Wear an apron.
4. Read the recipe all the way through before you start.
5. Get out all the ingredients and utensils listed in the recipe.

### WHILE YOU ARE COOKING
1. Put each ingredient away as soon as you are through with it.
2. Always use a pot holder for hot pans and pots.
3. Turn the handles of pots on the stove inward, away from the edge of the stove and away from you, so that you can't accidently knock them over.
4. If you have a timer in the kitchen, use it.

### WHEN YOU HAVE FINISHED
1. Wash the dishes.
2. Put everything away.
3. Wipe up counter tops, range top and sink.
4. Leave the kitchen in tip-top shape.

### REMEMBER
Any time you could use help from an older person, *ask* for help.
(Whatever trouble you're getting into could get worse!)

You may need help from an older person to:
1. Turn on the stove - burners, broiler, oven or microwave.
2. Cut or slice with knives.
3. Use any electrical appliance or equipment.
4. Remove hot stuff from the stove.
5. Carry something heavy.

## ALWAYS ASK FOR HELP IF YOU NEED IT!

# KITCHEN SAFETY

## FIRE

**Don't** cook when wearing shirts with long, baggy sleeves or with your hair hanging down in your face. You could catch on fire.

**Use** potholders when handling hot pots, pans, and dishes.

**Steam** burns. Be careful of escaping steam when lifting casserole or saucepan lids.

**Be very careful** of boiling water and other boiling liquids. They can cause very serious burns. Never heat a pan full of oil. Use very little oil at a time—like one or two tablespoons at most. It's much safer and much healthier.

**Smother** a pan fire by covering it with the pan lid. Do not lift a burning pan to try to move it and DO NOT POUR WATER OVER IT.

**Always** keep a container of baking sofa near the stove in case something catches on fire.

Baking soda can often prevent a fire from breakinq out.

## APPLIANCE

**Never** submerge an electrical appliance in water.

**Never** use appliances near the sink or other water sources.

**To clean** an appliance like an electric mixer, unplug it and remove the beaters and wash them. Wipe the mixer itself with a damp sponge or cloth, but don't wash it.

**Never** handle electrical appliances when your hands are wet. You could be shocked.

## KNIFE

**Always** use an appropriately sized knife. Usually a paring knife or a small slicing knife will fill most of your cooking needs.

**Pay attention** to what you are doing. Look at what you are doing.

**Never** use a dull knife, as this is more dangerous than using a sharp knife correctly.

**When walking** with a knife, keep the sharp end pointed down.

**Always** cut away from your hand when handling knives or blades. If the knife should slip, it will cut the food or cutting board, not you.

To be a good cook you *must* use the *right* tools and *measure* carefully.

**Measure liquids such as water, milk, and cooking oil in a clear measuring cup with a spout.**
- Place the cup on a counter top.
- "Bend down so your eye is even with the correct measuring line.
- Slowly fill the cup to the correct line.

**Measure dry and solid ingredients such as flour, sugar, shredded cheese and chopped vegetables with plastic or metal cups.**
- Choose the right size cup.
- Fill the cup to the top.
- Level it with the edge of a spatula.

**Measure soft margarine or brown sugar with plastic or metal cups.**
- Pack these foods firmly into a cup to force air out.
- Level it with the edge of a spatula.

**Measure small amounts of foods such as liquids, salt, spices, and flavorings in special measuring spoons, not the kind for eating.**
- Dip the right size spoon into the container or pour liquid into the spoon.
- Level dry foods with the edge of a spatula.

**Measure stick margarine** by placing on a cutting board and cutting off the amount you need with a small sharp knife. Amounts are clearly marked on the wrapper.

# TABLE OF MEASURES

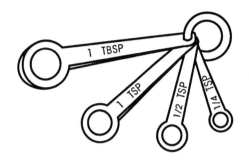

# "THIS" EQUALS "THAT"

| This | | That |
|---|---|---|
| 3 teaspoons | = | 1 Tablespoon |
| 4 Tablespoons | = | 1/4 cup |
| 5 Tablespoons + 1 teaspoon | = | 1/3 cup |
| 8 Tablespoons | | 1/2 cup |
| 16 Tablespoons | = | 1 cup |
| 1 cup | = | 8 ounces |
| 2 cups or 16 ounces | = | 1 pint |
| 4 cups or 32 ounces | = | 1 quart |
| 2 pints | = | 1 quart |
| 2 quarts | = | 1/2 gallon |
| 4 quarts | | 1 gallon |
| 16 ounces | = | 1 pound (dry weight) |
| 1/2 cup or 1/4 lb. or 8 Tablespoons | = | 1 stick butter or margarine |
| 60 minutes | = | 1 hour |
| few grains | = | less than 1/8 teaspoon |
| dash | = | 2-3 drops |

# ABBREVIATIONS

| | | |
|---|---|---|
| t. or tsp. | = | teaspoon |
| T. or Tbsp. | = | tablespoon |
| c. | = | cup |
| fg | = | few grains |
| pt. | = | pint |
| qt. | = | quart |
| gal. | = | gallon |
| oz. | = | ounces |
| lb. | = | pound |
| min. | = | minute |
| mod. | = | moderate |
| med. | = | medium |
| lg. | = | large |
| doz. | = | dozen |
| pkg. | = | package |

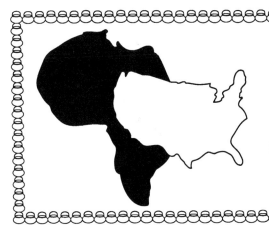

# BEVERAGES

## Good Things To Drink

Kool-Aid®
Lemonade
Iced Tea

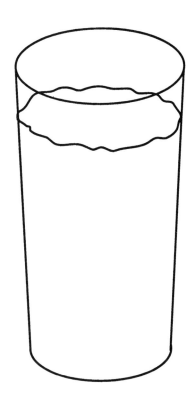

Hot Cocoa
Egg Nog (Adult)
Quick Egg Nog
(For Kids)

# KOOL-AID®

## The INGREDIENTS I need

1 pkg.   Kool-Aid®
1 cup   Sugar
8 cups   Cold Water
    Ice

## The EQUIPMENT I need

Pitcher
Measuring cup
Spoon

88888888888888888 **How To Make It** 888888888888888888

1. Empty Kool-Aid® into pitcher.
2. Add sugar, water and ice.
3. Stir well.

**Makes 2 quarts**

# LEMONADE

## The INGREDIENTS I need

| | |
|---|---|
| 6 | Lemons |
| 1 cup | Sugar |
| 8 cups | Cold Water |

## The EQUIPMENT I need

Pitcher
Measuring cup
Spoon

ଷଷଷଷଷଷଷଷଷଷଷଷଷଷଷ **How To Make It** ଷଷଷଷଷଷଷଷଷଷଷଷଷଷଷ

1. Roll the lemons on the table to loosen the juice.
2. Cut the lemons in half and squeeze the juice out.
3. Mix the sugar, lemon juice and cold water.
4. Serve in tall glasses over ice cubes.

**Makes 2 quarts**

# ICED TEA

## The INGREDIENTS I need

| | |
|---|---|
| 2 | Tea Bags |
| 2 cups | Boiling Water |
| 1/4 cup | Sugar |
| 2 cups | Cold Water |

## The EQUIPMENT I need

Pitcher
Measuring cup
Spoon

## ၆၆၆၆၆၆၆၆၆၆၆၆၆၆၆ How To Make It ၆၆၆၆၆၆၆၆၆၆၆၆၆၆၆

1. Pour boiling water into pitcher with tea bags.
2. Let set for 10 minutes. Remove tea bags.
3. Stir in sugar.
4. Add cold water.
5. Stir well.
6. Serve in tall glass with ice cubes and lemon wedge or mint sprigs.

Serves 4

# HOT COCOA

## The INGREDIENTS I need

| | |
|---|---|
| 1 cup | Boiling Water |
| 3 Tbsp. | Cocoa |
| 3 Tbsp. | Sugar |
| 3 cups | Milk |

## The EQUIPMENT I need

Saucepan
Measuring cup/spoons
Wooden spoon

## ᪣᪣᪣᪣᪣᪣᪣᪣᪣᪣᪣᪣᪣ How To Make It ᪣᪣᪣᪣᪣᪣᪣᪣᪣᪣᪣᪣᪣

1. Combine boiling water, cocoa and sugar in saucepan.
2. Cook over low heat until smooth.
3. Place milk in separate saucepan and scald.
4. Add milk to cocoa mixture, stir until smooth.
5. Pour cocoa mixture into hot milk.
6. Beat with spoon.
7. Serve with whipped cream or marshmallow dropped in to float on top.

**Serves 4**

# EGG NOG (ADULT)

## The INGREDIENTS I need

| 6 | Eggs, separated |
| 6 T. | Sugar |
| 6 T. | Bourbon (Optional) |
| 6 T. | Rum or Rum Flavor (Optional) |
| 1pint | Heavy Cream, whipped |
| 1tsp. | Vanilla |
| 1tsp. | Nutmeg |

## The EQUIPMENT I need

Measuring spoons
Egg beater or electric mixer
Bowl

NOTE! This recipe is for grown-ups to drink. Make sure you have permission to make this before you start. It is also a good idea to have your grown-up helper handle the alcohol.

ଌଌଌଌଌଌଌଌଌଌଌଌଌଌ **How To Make It** ଌଌଌଌଌଌଌଌଌଌଌଌଌଌ

1. Beat egg whites until stiff.
2. Beat egg yolks, vanilla and sugar until eggs are light in color.
3. (Optional) Gradually add bourbon and rum, beating all the time.
4. Fold in egg whites and then the whipped cream.
5. Sprinkle with nutmeg and chill.

**Serves 8-10**

# QUICK EGG NOG (For Kids)

## The INGREDIENTS I need

1(12-oz.) Container of
        Whipped Topping with
        Real Cream (4-1/2 c.)
6        Eggs
1        Cup Milk
2 T.     Sugar
2 tsp.   Vanilla
1/4 tsp. Nutmeg

## The EQUIPMENT I need

Measuring cup/spoons
Blender
Bowl

### ଚଚଚଚଚଚଚଚଚଚଚଚଚ How To Make It ଚଚଚଚଚଚଚଚଚଚଚଚଚ

1. Place 3 cups whipped topping and remaining ingredients in blender.
2. Cover and process on high speed until well blended.
3. Pour into bowl.
4. Top with remaining whipped topping.

**Serves 6-8**

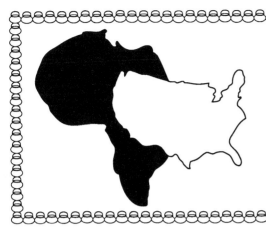

# BREADS, ROLLS AND BISCUITS

## *Homemade!*

Baking Powder Biscuits
Buttermilk Biscuits
Homemade Cornbread
Jiffy Cornbread Muffins
Corn Pone
Cracklin' Bread

Dinner Rolls
Garlic Bread
Hoe Cakes

Hot Water Cornbread
Hush Puppies
Monkey Bread
Refrigerator Rolls
Spoon Bread

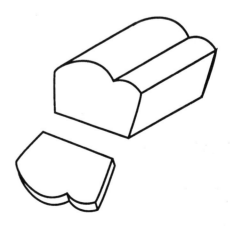

# BAKING POWDER BISCUITS

## The INGREDIENTS I need

| | |
|---|---|
| 2 cups | Flour |
| 4 tsp. | Baking Powder |
| 1 tsp. | Salt |
| 4 Tbsp. | Shortening |
| 2/3 cup | Milk |

## The EQUIPMENT I need

Measuring cup/spoons
Bowl
Fork
Sifter
Board
Rolling pin
Biscuit cutter
Cookie sheet

## 88888888888888888 How To Make It 88888888888888888

1. Sift flour, baking powder and salt together in bowl.
2. Add shortening into flour mix.
3. Add milk into flour mix.
4. Stir with a fork just enough to make a soft dough. (Knead 8 times).
5. Roll dough on floured board to 1/2 inch thick.
6. Cut out with a biscuit cutter.
7. Place biscuits on baking sheet side by side.
8. Bake at 400 degrees for 15 minutes.

Makes 12

# BUTTERMILK BISCUITS

## The INGREDIENTS I need

| | |
|---|---|
| 2-1/2 cups | Flour |
| 1 Tbsp. | Baking Powder |
| 1 tsp. | Salt |
| 1/2 tsp. | Baking Soda |
| 1/4 cup | Shortening |
| 1 cup | Buttermilk |

## The EQUIPMENT I need

Measuring cup/spoons
Fork
Sifter
Board
Rolling pin
Biscuit cutter
Cookie sheet

## ᪗᪗᪗᪗᪗᪗᪗᪗᪗᪗᪗᪗᪗᪗᪗ How To Make It ᪗᪗᪗᪗᪗᪗᪗᪗᪗᪗᪗᪗᪗᪗᪗

1. Preheat oven to 400 degrees.
2. Sift together flour, baking powder, salt and baking soda.
3. Cut in shortening, using a fork.
4. Add milk and stir until a soft dough forms.
5. Turn onto lightly floured board.
6. Knead until smooth.
7. Roll out to 1/2 inch thickness.
8. Cut with biscuit cutter or the rim of a glass.
9. Place biscuits on greased cookie sheet, just touching.
10. Bake for 15 minutes.

**Makes 12-15**

# HOMEMADE CORNBREAD

## The INGREDIENTS I need

| | |
|---|---|
| 1 cup | Flour |
| 1 cup | Yellow Cornmeal |
| 1 Tbsp. | Baking Powder |
| 1-1/2 tsp. | Salt |
| 1-1/2 tsp. | Sugar |
| 1 cup | Milk |
| 2 | Eggs, beaten |
| 1/3 cup | Vegetable Oil |

## The EQUIPMENT I need

Bowl
Egg Beater
Measuring cup/spoons
8" Square pan or
Muffin pan

8888888888888888 **How To Make It** 8888888888888888

1. In bowl beat together eggs.
2. Add sugar, milk and oil.
3. Add dry ingredients—flour, cornmeal, baking powder and salt.
4. Beat well until slightly lumpy.
5. Pour mixture into greased pan or muffin pan.
6. Bake at 400 degrees for 30 minutes.

**Serves 6**

# JIFFY CORNBREAD MUFFINS

## The INGREDIENTS I need

1 pkg.   Corn Muffin Mix
1        Egg
1/3 cup  Milk

## The EQUIPMENT I need

Muffin Pan
Bowl
Spoon
Pam

## &&&&&&&&&&&&&&&& How To Make It &&&&&&&&&&&&&&&&

1. Preheat over to 400 degrees
2. Blend all the ingredients together.
3. Spray muffin pan with Pam or grease lightly.
4. Fill muffin cups 1/2 full.
5. Bake 15 to 20 minutes or until golden brown.

Makes 12 muffins

# CORN PONE

## The INGREDIENTS I need

| | |
|---|---|
| 3 cups | Cornmeal |
| 2 tsp. | Salt |
| 1-1/4 cups | Boiling Water |
| 1 tsp. | Vegetable Oil |
| 2 | Eggs |
| 1 cup | Cream |
| 2 tsp. | Baking Powder |

## The EQUIPMENT I need

Measuring cup/spoons
Pot
Bowl
Wooden spoon
Baking sheet

ꙮꙮꙮꙮꙮꙮꙮꙮꙮꙮꙮꙮꙮ **How To Make It** ꙮꙮꙮꙮꙮꙮꙮꙮꙮꙮꙮꙮꙮ

1. Mix cornmeal and salt together in bowl.
2. Add oil.
3. Pour into boiling water and stir until well-mixed, (Stiff batter).
4. Add eggs and cream. Cool for 30 minutes or when the butter is cool enough to handle.
5. Add baking powder and mix well.
6. Shape dough into pones, (oblong cakes about 5 inches long, 3 inches wide and 3/4 inches thick).
7. Drop on baking sheet and bake at 400 degrees for 30 minutes.

**Serves 4-6**

- - - - - - - - - - - - - - - - - - - - - - - - - - - - - - - - - - - - - - - - *HOMEMADE!*

# CRACKLIN' BREAD

## The INGREDIENTS I need

| | |
|---|---|
| 2 cups | Yellow Cornmeal |
| 1-1/2 tsp. | Baking Powder |
| 1/2 tsp. | Baking Soda |
| 1-1/2 tsp. | Salt |
| *1/2 cup | Crackling |
| 1 cup | Buttermilk |
| 2 | Eggs, beaten |
| 2 Tbsp. | Bacon Dripping |

## The EQUIPMENT I need

Measuring cup/spoons
Sifter
Bowl
Wooden spoon
8" square baking pan
Rubber spatula

## ꙮꙮꙮꙮꙮꙮꙮꙮꙮꙮꙮꙮꙮ How To Make It ꙮꙮꙮꙮꙮꙮꙮꙮꙮꙮꙮꙮꙮ

1. Preheat oven to 400 degrees.
2. Sift cornmeal, baking powder, baking soda and salt together.
3. Add crackling, buttermilk, eggs and bacon dripping; mix well.
4. Spread in a greased 8 inch square baking pan.
5. Bake for 25-30 minutes.

Serves 4-6

*Crackling - To make fresh crackling, cut the fat off of any fresh uncooked pork, ham or roast. Cut the fat into very small cubes. Fry it over low heat until the fat has rendered, and the cracklings are golden brown. Do not burn.

# DINNER ROLLS

## The INGREDIENTS I need

| | |
|---|---|
| 2 pkgs. | Dried Active Yeast |
| 1/2 cup | Lukewarm Water |
| 3/4 cup | Scalded Milk |
| 1/4 cup | Vegetable Shortening |
| 3/4 tsp. | Salt |
| 1/4 cup | Sugar |
| 1 | Egg, beaten |
| 3-4 cups | Flour, sifted |

## The EQUIPMENT I need

Baking pan
Measuring cup/spoons
Dish towel for cover
Cutting board

## How To Make It

1. Dissolve yeast in lukewarm water.
2. In a bowl, blend scalded milk, shortening, salt and sugar. Let cool. Add eggs.
3. Add half of the flour. Mix well. Add enough of the remaining flour to handle dough without it sticking to your hands.
4. Cover bowl for 15 minutes.
5. On well floured board, shape dough into rolls. Cover after placing rolls in an ungreased baking pan.
6. Allow 1 hour for it to rise in a warm place until it is double in size.
7. Bake at 400 degrees for 15-20 minutes.

**Makes 18 rolls**

 *HOMEMADE!*

# GARLIC BREAD

## The INGREDIENTS I need

| | |
|---|---|
| 1 loaf | French Bread |
| 3 T. | Butter or Margarine |
| 1 tsp. | Garlic Powder |

## The EQUIPMENT I need

Knife
Foil

∂∂∂∂∂∂∂∂∂∂∂∂∂∂∂∂ **How To Make It** ∂∂∂∂∂∂∂∂∂∂∂∂∂∂∂∂

1. Make deep slits across the French bread.
2. Butter each side of slits with softened butter.
3. Sprinkle with garlic powder.
4. Wrap in foil.
5. Heat on grill or 350° oven for 15 minutes.

Serves 4-6

# HOE CAKES

## The INGREDIENTS I need

| | |
|---|---|
| 1 cup | White Cornmeal |
| 1/2 tsp. | Salt |
| 3/4 cup | Boiling Water |
| 2 Tbsp. | Bacon fat, Butter or Vegetable Oil |

## The EQUIPMENT I need

Skillet
Pot
Bowl
Measuring cup/spoons
Wooden spoon
Tablespoon
Spatula

## ୫୫୫୫୫୫୫୫୫୫୫୫୫୫ How To Make It ୫୫୫୫୫୫୫୫୫୫୫୫୫୫

1. Mix meal and salt in bowl.
2. Add boiling water. Stir constantly with spoon; mix well.
3. Beat until smooth soft dough.
4. Drop rounded tablespoonfuls of dough into hot oil.
5. Spread to form flat circles.
6. Cook until golden brown (2 minutes) on each side, turning once with spatula.
7. Drain on paper towel. Serve hot.

**Makes 8**

*HOMEMADE!*

# HOT WATER CORNBREAD

## The INGREDIENTS I need

| | |
|---|---|
| 1 Cup | White Cornmeal |
| 2 cups | Hot Water |
| 1 tsp. | Sugar |
| 1/2 tsp. | Salt |
| 1/2 tsp. | Baking Powder |

## The EQUIPMENT I need

Bowl
Wooden spoon
Measuring cup/spoons
Pot
Skillet

8888888888888888 **How To Make It** 8888888888888888

1. Mix cornmeal, sugar, salt and baking powder together.
2. Bring water to a boil in a pot.
3. Add 1/2 cup of water and mix well.
4. Add more water if needed for thick batter.
5. Spoon and pat into patties.
6. Deep fry in hot oil until brown.

Serves 2-4

# HUSH PUPPIES

## The INGREDIENTS I need

| | |
|---|---|
| 1 cup | Cornmeal |
| 3/4 cup | Flour |
| 2 tsp. | Baking Powder |
| 1 | Egg |
| 3/4 cup | Milk |
| 1/2 cup | Onion, chopped |
| 1 tsp. | Salt |
| 1/4 cup | Oil |

## The EQUIPMENT I need

Measuring cup/spoons
Bowl
Cutting board/knife
Skillet

## ठठठठठठठठठठठठठठ How To Make It ठठठठठठठठठठठठठठ

1. Mix cornmeal, flour, baking powder and salt together.
2. Beat together milk, eggs and onion.
3. Add all the ingredients together and mix well.
4. Shape into small balls.
5. Drop into skillet.
6. Cook until golden brown.

**Serves 4**

# MONKEY BREAD

## The INGREDIENTS I need

| | |
|---|---|
| 1 cup | Milk |
| 1 cup | Butter |
| 1/3 cup | Shortening |
| 1 tsp. | Salt |
| 3 | Eggs, beaten |
| 2 pkgs. | Yeast (or cakes) |
| 1/4 cup | Warm Water |
| 1 Tbsp. | Sugar |
| 4 cups | Flour |

## The EQUIPMENT I need

Pot
10" tube or mold pan
Measuring cup/spoons
Bowl
Wooden spoon
Rolling pin
Biscuit cutter
Dish towel (for cover)

## ᙚᙚᙚᙚᙚᙚᙚᙚᙚᙚᙚᙚᙚᙚᙚ How To Make It ᙚᙚᙚᙚᙚᙚᙚᙚᙚᙚᙚᙚᙚᙚᙚ

1. Scald milk, shortening, salt and 1/2 cup butter or margarine. Cool to lukewarm.
2. Soften yeast in warm water and stir in sugar.
3. Stir beaten eggs and lukewarm milk mixture into yeast mixture.
4. Gradually beat in flour with wooden spoon to make a soft dough that clings together: knead lightly.
5. Put dough in a bowl and cover and let rise, until doubled in size.
6. Divide in half, roll out on floured board to about 1/3 inch thick
7. Melt remaining 1/2 cup butter.
8. Cut dough into 3-inch diamond shapes or with a floured biscuit cutter and overlap each biscuit.
9. Dip pieces of dough into melted butter.
10. Layer into a greased 10-inch mold or tube pan. You should have 3 layers. Don't fill pan more than 3/4 full.
11. Cover and let rise again for 1 hour. Bake at 375 degrees for 15 minutes.
12. Turn out onto serving plate. Pull apart.

**Serves 10-12**

# REFRIGERATOR ROLLS

## The INGREDIENTS I need

| | |
|---|---|
| 1 cup | Milk |
| 2 sticks | Butter |
| 1 cup | Sugar |
| 6 cups | Flour |
| 4 | Eggs, well beaten |
| 2 pkg. | Yeast |
| 1/2 cup | Lukewarm Water |
| 4 tsp. | Salt |

## The EQUIPMENT I need

Large bowl
Pot
Measuring cup/spoons
Rolling pin
Biscuit cutter
Pastry brush
Baking sheet or pan
Timer

## How To Make It

1. Scald the milk and add the butter, sugar and salt and stir until dissolved.
2. Pour the mixture into a large bowl ad let it cool.
3. Add the eggs and yeast, pre-dissolved in water.
4. Mix the flour, 3 cups at a time, into the mixture.
5. Let the dough rise in a warm place until it is doubled in bulk.
6. Push it down and refrigerate overnight.
7. NEXT DAY: Roll out the dough on a floured board.
8. Cut it with a biscuit cutter.
9. Brush the tops with melted butter.
10. Fold over and top with more butter.
11. Let the dough rise again, twice its size.
12. Bake at 375 degrees until brown.
13. Rolls can be frozen.

Makes 3 dozen

*HOMEMADE!*

# SPOON BREAD

## The INGREDIENTS I need

| | |
|---|---|
| 1 cup | Yellow Cornmeal |
| 1-1/2 cup | Boiling Water |
| 1 cup | Milk |
| 3 Tbsp. | Butter |
| 1 tsp. | Salt |
| 2 | Eggs, beaten |

## The EQUIPMENT I need

Bowl
Pot
Casserole pan
Measuring cup/spoons
Wooden spoon

## ∞∞∞∞∞∞∞∞∞∞∞∞∞∞ How To Make It ∞∞∞∞∞∞∞∞∞∞∞∞∞∞

1. Preheat oven to 375 degrees.
2. Combine cornmeal and boiling water, stir until smooth.
3. Add butter and salt; mix well.
4. Let cool.
5. Add milk and beaten eggs.
6. Pour into greased casserole.
7. Bake at 375 degrees for 30 minutes.

Serves 6

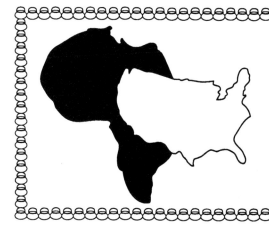

# BREAKFAST

## *Traditional Southern Recipes*

Bacon
Cheese Toast
Eggs (Hardboiled)
Eggs (Fried)
Eggs (Scrambled)
French Toast
Fried Apples
Grits
Ham
Home Fried Potatoes
Pancakes
Sausage
Soda Biscuits
Waffles

# BACON

## The INGREDIENTS I need

Bacon

## The EQUIPMENT I need

Pan/wire rack/microwave

∞∞∞∞∞∞∞∞∞∞∞∞∞∞∞ **How To Make It** ∞∞∞∞∞∞∞∞∞∞∞∞∞∞∞

**Baking:**

Place strips of bacon in shallow pan and cook in hot oven until browned.

**Broiling:**

Place slices of bacon on wire rack over dripping pan. Broil under hot fire and when one side of bacon is browned, turn and brown other side.

**Microwave:**

Cook bacon on bacon rack with paper towel. To avoid spattering, microwave on 100% power. Microwave one minute for each slice bacon.

**Pan Broiling:**

Place strips of cold bacon in cold frying pan over low fire and cook slowly. Never let bacon remain in fat, but pour off excess fat from time to time. Turn frequently increasing heat until bacon is crisp.

# CHEESE TOAST

## The INGREDIENTS I need

4 slices    White or Wheat bread
1 Tbsp.    Butter
              or Margarine
4 slices    American Cheese

## The EQUIPMENT I need

Cookie sheet
Measuring spoon

Butter knife

888888888888888888 **How To Make It** 888888888888888888

1. Place bread on cookie sheet.
2. Spread butter or margarine on bread.
3. Place slice of cheese on buttered side of each.
4. Bake at 350 degrees for 3 minutes or until cheese has melted.

Serves 4

# EGGS (HARDBOILED)

## The INGREDIENTS I need

2        Eggs
Pinch    Salt

## The EQUIPMENT I need

Pot

8888888888888888 **How To Make It** 8888888888888888

1. Place 2 eggs in cold salted water to cover.
2. Bring to boiling and simmer 20 minutes.
3. Remove pan from heat.
4. Place under cold water.

**Serves 2**

# EGGS (FRIED)

## The INGREDIENTS I need

| | |
|---|---|
| 2 | Eggs |
| 1 Tbsp. | Butter or Margarine |
| Dash | Salt and Pepper |

## The EQUIPMENT I need

Skillet
Spatula

Spoon

ꝰꝰꝰꝰꝰꝰꝰꝰꝰꝰꝰꝰꝰꝰꝰ **How To Make It** ꝰꝰꝰꝰꝰꝰꝰꝰꝰꝰꝰꝰꝰꝰꝰ

1. Melt 1 tablespoon of butter or margarine in frying pan.
2. Break 2 eggs into pan one at a time.
3. Cool over low heat until whites are just set (5 minutes).
4. Spoon butter or margarine over top of eggs to cook thoroughly the part of the egg whites surrounding the yolks.
5. Sprinkle with salt and pepper.

**Serves 2**

# EGGS (SCRAMBLED)

## The INGREDIENTS I need

5 Eggs Large
1/4 cup Milk
1/2 tsp. Salt
2 Tbsp. Butter
         or Margarine

## The EQUIPMENT I need

Skillet
Bowl
Fork
Measuring cup/spoons

88888888888888888 **How To Make It** 8888888888888888

1. Break eggs into mixing bowl.
2. Add milk and salt. Beat with fork a few minutes.
3. Melt margarine or butter in frying pan over low heat.
4. Pour egg mixture into pan.
5. Stir away from bottom and sides of pan as eggs cook.
6. Cook until eggs are thick, 3-5 minutes.

**Serves 4**

# FRENCH TOAST

## The INGREDIENTS I need

| | |
|---|---|
| 1 | Egg |
| 4 Tbsp. | Milk |
| 1 tsp. | Sugar |
| Dash | Cinnamon or Nutmeg |
| 2 slices | Bread |
| 2 Tbsp. | Butter or Margarine |

## The EQUIPMENT I need

Measuring cup/spoons
Bowl
Skillet or pan
Fork

## ᗺᗺᗺᗺᗺᗺᗺᗺᗺᗺᗺᗺᗺᗺᗺᗺ How To Make It ᗺᗺᗺᗺᗺᗺᗺᗺᗺᗺᗺᗺᗺᗺᗺᗺ

1. Beat egg and milk lightly together.
2. Add sugar and cinnamon or nutmeg.
3. Mix well.
4. Coat slices of bread on both sides.
5. Brown lightly in hot butter or margarine.
6. Serve with powdered sugar and syrup.

Serves 1-2

# FRIED APPLES

## The INGREDIENTS I need

4           Green Apples
1/3 cup     Sugar
2 Tbsp.     Butter or Bacon Fat
2 Tbsp.     Water

## The EQUIPMENT I need

Apple peeler
Measuring cup/spoons
Skillet
Knife
Wooden spoon

ꙮꙮꙮꙮꙮꙮꙮꙮꙮꙮꙮꙮꙮꙮ **How To Make It** ꙮꙮꙮꙮꙮꙮꙮꙮꙮꙮꙮꙮꙮꙮ

1. Peel and core apples.
2. Cut into circles or slices.
3. Heat butter or bacon fat in skillet.
4. Add apples, sugar and water to skillet.
5. Stir and cook with the cover on.
6. Cook until apples are brown and liquid has dried up, (syrupy).

Serves 4

# GRITS

## The INGREDIENTS I need

1 cup    Grits
1 tsp.    Salt
4 cups    Water
3 Tbsp.    Butter or Margarine

## The EQUIPMENT I need

Pot
Measuring cup/spoons

ᘓᘓᘓᘓᘓᘓᘓᘓᘓᘓᘓᘓᘓᘓᘓ **How To Make It** ᘓᘓᘓᘓᘓᘓᘓᘓᘓᘓᘓᘓᘓᘓᘓ

1. Bring water to a boil.
2. Add salt.
3. Slowly stir in grits.
4. Stir constantly to prevent lumping.
5. Reduce heat and cover for 10 minutes.
6. Serve hot with butter.

**Serves 4**

# HAM

## The INGREDIENTS I need

| | |
|---|---|
| 3 | Boiled or baked Ham slices about 1/2 inch thick |
| 1 Tbsp. | Oil or Bacon Fat |

## The EQUIPMENT I need

Skillet
Measuring spoon

ଚଚଚଚଚଚଚଚଚଚଚଚଚଚ **How To Make It** ଚଚଚଚଚଚଚଚଚଚଚଚଚ

1. Heat the oil or bacon fat in skillet.
2. Add the ham slices.
3. Fry until crisp and lightly browned on both sides.

Serves 2-3

# HOME FRIED POTATOES

## The INGREDIENTS I need

| | |
|---|---|
| 3 large | White Potatoes, peeled and sliced |
| 2 medium | Onions, peeled and sliced |
| | Salt and Pepper to taste |
| 2 Tbsp. | Oil |

## The EQUIPMENT I need

Skillet
Cutting board/knife
Measuring spoon
Spatula
Bowl

## How To Make It

1. Peel and slice potatoes and onions.
2. Soak in cold water for 30 minutes. Drain.
3. Mix slices up in a bowl and add salt and pepper to taste.
4. Heat the oil in a skillet.
5. Put in potatoes and onions; cover and cook slowly for 15 minutes.
6. Uncover and turn over with spatula.
7. Cover and cook about 15 minutes more.
8. Potatoes are done when tender in the center and light brown and crisp on the outside.

Serves 4

# PANCAKES

## The INGREDIENTS I need

| | |
|---|---|
| 1 cup | Milk |
| 2 Tbsp. | melted Butter or Margarine |
| 1 | Egg, beaten |
| 1 cup | Flour |
| 2 tsp. | Baking Powder |
| 1-1/2 Tbsp. | Sugar |
| 1/2 tsp. | Salt |

## The EQUIPMENT I need

Skillet or griddle
Measuring cup/spoons

Sifter
Bowl
Spatula
Wooden spoon

## ꧁꧁꧁꧁꧁꧁꧁꧁꧁꧁ How To Make It ꧁꧁꧁꧁꧁꧁꧁꧁꧁꧁

1. Sift the dry ingredients together into a bowl.
2. Mix the egg, milk and butter or margarine.
3. Add to dry ingredients.
4. Stir until the flour is moistened (the batter will be lumpy).
5. Fry on a hot skillet or griddle (grease very lightly with a vegetable Spray.)
6. Drop the batter by tablespoonfuls or 1/4 cupfuls.
7. Cook until the top side of the cake is full of bubbles and the underside is nicely browned.
8. Turn cake over and brown the other side.

**Makes 4 cakes**

# SAUSAGE

## The INGREDIENTS I need

6 Link   Sausages
1/4 cup   Water

## The EQUIPMENT I need

Frying pan/lid
Measuring cup
Tongs or fork
Paper towels

&#10216;&#10216;&#10216;&#10216;&#10216;&#10216;&#10216;&#10216;&#10216; How To Make It &#10216;&#10216;&#10216;&#10216;&#10216;&#10216;&#10216;&#10216;&#10216;

1. Put the frying pan over medium heat and pour in 1/4 cup of water.
2. Put the sausages into the pan and cover.
3. Let the water boil until it disappears and then let the sausages brown - 10 minutes.
4. Remove the lid and turn the sausages so that they will brown on all sides. They must be cooked thoroughly. (This is very important with pork).
5. Take the sausages out of the pan with the fork or tongs and drain them on the paper towels.

Serves 2-3

MICROWAVE Instructions:
1. Cook sausage on rack with paper towel.
2. 4 links:  2-1/2 to 3 1/2 minutes
   4 Brown and Serve:  1-1/2 to 2 minutes

# SODA BISCUITS

## The INGREDIENTS I need

| | |
|---|---|
| 2 cups | Flour |
| 2 tsp. | Cream of Tartar |
| 2 Tbsp. | Crisco |
| 1/2 tsp. | Baking Soda |
| 1/2 tsp. | Salt |
| 1 cup | Milk |

## The EQUIPMENT I need

Measuring cup/spoons
Sifter
Bowl
Rolling pin
Biscuit cutter
Baking sheet

## ⌢⌢⌢⌢⌢⌢⌢⌢⌢⌢⌢⌢⌢⌢⌢⌢⌢ How To Make It ⌢⌢⌢⌢⌢⌢⌢⌢⌢⌢⌢⌢⌢⌢⌢⌢

1. Combine flour with cream of tartar and salt.
2. Sift together into mixing bowl.
3. Cut in the shortening.
4. Dissolve soda in milk and stir into flour mixture, mixing as little as possible.
5. Turn out onto floured surface and roll out to 1-inch thickness.
6. Cut into rounds with biscuit cutter and arrange on greased baking sheet.
7. Bake at 450 degrees until lightly browned.

**Makes 12-15**

# WAFFLES

## The INGREDIENTS I need

| | |
|---|---|
| 2 cups | Flour |
| 2 tsp. | Baking Powder |
| 1/2 tsp. | Baking Soda |
| 1/2 tsp. | Salt |
| 1 Tbsp. | Sugar |
| 3 | Eggs, separated |
| 1/3 cup | Melted Margarine |
| 1-1/2 cup | Milk |

## The EQUIPMENT I need

Waffle iron
Measuring cup/spoons
Bowl
Wooden spoon
Egg beater or electric mixer
Wire whisk
Sifter

ꕤꕤꕤꕤꕤꕤꕤꕤꕤꕤꕤꕤꕤꕤ **How To Make It** ꕤꕤꕤꕤꕤꕤꕤꕤꕤꕤꕤꕤꕤꕤ

1. Sift flour, baking powder, baking soda, sugar and salt together.
2. Combine beaten egg yolks, margarine and milk.
3. Add to dry ingredients, mixing well.
4. Beat egg whites with wire whisk until stiff but not dry.
5. Fold into batter.
6. Pour a thin coat of batter onto hot waffle iron.
7. Bake 15 to 18 minutes.

**Makes 6-8**

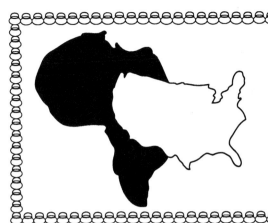

# SOUPS

## *Good for the Soul*

Bean Soup
Chicken Noodle (with Chicken Stock)
Down Home Vegetable Soup
Oxtail Soup
Turkey Soup

# BEAN SOUP

## The INGREDIENTS I need

| | |
|---|---|
| 1 cup | Lima or Navy beans, dried |
| 6 cups | Water, cold |
| 1 | Ham Bone or Smoked Turkey |
| 1 med. | Onion, chopped |
| 1 cup | Celery, chopped |
| 1/2 cup | Carrots |
| 1/2 tsp. | Salt |
| 1/4 tsp. | Pepper |
| 1 | Bay Leaf |

## The EQUIPMENT I need

Pot/lid
Measuring cup/spoons
Cutting board/knife

## ꙮꙮꙮꙮꙮꙮꙮꙮꙮꙮꙮꙮꙮꙮꙮ How To Make It ꙮꙮꙮꙮꙮꙮꙮꙮꙮꙮꙮꙮꙮꙮꙮ

1. Add beans to pot with cold water.
2. Bring to a boil. Reduce heat to low.
3. Add meat, salt, pepper, onions, bay leaf and celery.
4. Simmer slowly until beans are tender—about 2 1/2 hours.
5. Add the carrots and cook 30 minutes more.
6. Remove bay leaf.

**Serves 6**

# CHICKEN NOODLE SOUP

## The INGREDIENTS I need

| | |
|---|---|
| 2-3 pound | Chicken, cut up |
| 10 cups | Water |
| 2 Cubes | Chicken Bouillon |
| 1 cup | Onions, chopped |
| 1/2 tsp. | Salt |
| 1/2 tsp. | Pepper |
| 1 | Bay Leaf |
| 1 cup | Celery, sliced |
| 1 cup | Carrots, thinly sliced |
| 2 cups | Wide Egg Noodles |

## The EQUIPMENT I need

Large Pot/lid
Measuring cup/spoons
Cutting board/knife

## How To Make It

1. Combine chicken and water in pot.
2. Bring to a boil. Reduce heat, cover and simmer 15 minutes.
3. Add bouillon cubes, salt, pepper and bay leaf to pot. Simmer 30 minutes until chicken is tender then skim fat from broth and return chicken to broth.
4. Remove chicken from broth, cut into bite size pieces.
5. Stir in celery, carrots and onions
6. Simmer and cover for 15 minutes.
7. Remove bay leaf.
8. Drop noodles into boiling soup for 5 to 10 minutes.

**Serves 8**

# CHICKEN STOCK

## The INGREDIENTS I need

| | |
|---|---|
| 1 | Whole Chicken |
| 1 | Onion, chopped |
| 3 | Celery Stalks, chopped |
| 2 | Carrots, chopped |
| 2 | Bay Leaves |
| 5 quarts | Water |

## The EQUIPMENT I need

2-Gallon Pot
Cutting board/knife

## ≋≋≋≋≋≋≋≋≋≋≋≋≋≋≋ How To Make It ≋≋≋≋≋≋≋≋≋≋≋≋≋≋≋

1. Put all ingredients in a 2-gallon pot.
2. Simmer for 2 hours.
3. Remove chicken and strain.

Makes 4 quarts

# DOWN HOME VEGETABLE SOUP

## The INGREDIENTS I need

| | |
|---|---|
| 1 | Soup Bone |
| 4 cups | Water |
| 1 medium | Onion, chopped |
| 3 stalks | Celery and leaves, chopped |
| 3 | Carrots, sliced |
| 1 tsp. | Salt |
| 1/4 tsp. | Pepper |
| 4 | Potatoes, peeled and quartered |
| 1/2 cup | Corn |
| 1/2 cup | Peas |

## The EQUIPMENT I need

Pot/lid
Measuring cup/spoons
Cutting board/knife

## &&&&&&&&&&&&&&&& How To Make It &&&&&&&&&&&&&&&&

1. Place all ingredients in a large pot.
2. Bring to a boil. Lower heat.
3. Cover pot and simmer for 1 hour.

Serves 2-6

# OXTAIL SOUP

## The INGREDIENTS I need

| | |
|---|---|
| 2 small | Oxtail |
| 1/4 tsp. | Salt |
| 1/4 tsp. | Pepper |
| 1/4 cup | Flour |
| 3 Tbsp. | Butter or Margarine |
| 6 cups | Beef or Chicken Stock |
| | (3 bouillon cubes dissolved in water) |
| 1/2 cup | Onion chopped |
| 1/2 cup | Celery, chopped |
| 1 cup | Potatoes, diced |
| 1 pkg. | Frozen String Beans |
| 1 pkg. | Frozen Peas and Carrots |
| 1 pkg. | Frozen Lima Beans |
| 1 pkg. | Frozen Okra (optional) |
| 1 tsp. | Worcestershire Sauce |
| 1 can | Tomatoes, large size |

## The EQUIPMENT I need

Pot/lid
Skillet
Measuring cup/spoons
Cutting board/knife
Can Opener

## ඍඍඍඍඍඍඍඍඍඍඍඍඍඍ How To Make It ඍඍඍඍඍඍඍඍඍඍඍඍඍඍ

1. Cut oxtail into small pieces. Wash well and drain.
2. Sprinkle with salt and pepper and dredge in flour.
3. Fry in butter or margarine for 10 minutes.
4. Add stock and simmer 2 hours or until tender.
5. Add vegetables to stock for 30 minutes.
6. Simmer until vegetables are soft.

Serves 4-6

# TURKEY SOUP

## The INGREDIENTS I need

| | |
|---|---|
| 1 | Turkey Carcass, (Bones and trimmings) |
| 8 cups | Water |
| 3 cubes | Chicken Bouillon |
| 1 tsp. | Salt |
| 1/4 tsp. | Poultry Seasoning |
| 1 | Bay Leaf |
| 1-1/2 cups | Carrots, sliced |
| 1 cup | Onions, chopped |
| 1 cup | Celery |
| 1/2 cup | Rice, uncooked  or |
| 1-1/2 cups | Wide Egg Noodles |

## The EQUIPMENT I need

Large pot/lid
Measuring cup/spoons
Cutting board/knife

## ଷଷଷଷଷଷଷଷଷଷଷଷଷଷଷ How To Make It ଷଷଷଷଷଷଷଷଷଷଷଷଷଷ

1. Combine turkey bones and trimmings, water, bouillon cubes, salt, poultry seasoning and bay leaf to pot.
2. Bring to boil. Cover and simmer for 1 hour.
3. Remove bones from broth. Remove turkey from bones.
4. Skim off fat. Return turkey to broth.
5. Stir in carrots, onions and celery and simmer for 20 minutes.
6. Add rice or noodles into boiling soup for 15-25 minutes until done.
7. Remove bay leaf.

Serves 8

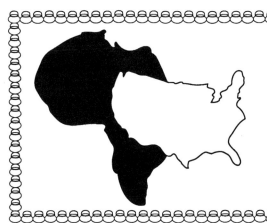

# SALADS

## *Fresh from the Garden*

Coleslaw

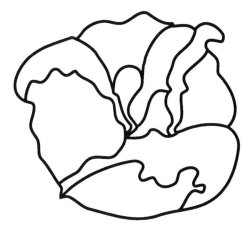

Cucumber

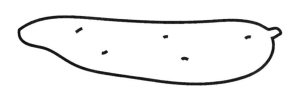

Carrot

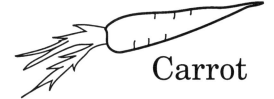

Potato

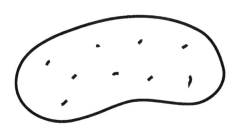

Macaroni

Tossed Green Salad

# AMBROSIA

## The INGREDIENTS I need

| | |
|---|---|
| 5 large | Oranges, peeled and sectioned |
| 1 8-oz. can | Pineapple Chunks |
| 1 cup | Shredded Coconut |
| 2 | Bananas, sliced (optional) |
| 1/3 cup | Cherries, pitted (optional) |
| 1/4 cup | Sugar to taste |
| 1/3 cup | Pecans or Walnuts, chopped (optional) |

## The EQUIPMENT I need

Knife/Cutting board
Can opener
Measuring cups
Bowl
Spoon

## ଚ୧ଚ୧ଚ୧ଚ୧ଚ୧ଚ୧ଚ୧ଚ୧ How To Make It ଚ୧ଚ୧ଚ୧ଚ୧ଚ୧ଚ୧ଚ୧ଚ୧

1. Peel oranges with knife.
2. Add undrained pineapple.
3. Stir in coconut and nuts.
4. Add sugar to taste.
5. Add bananas and cherries.
6. Refrigerate overnight.

**Serves 6-8**

# CABBAGE SLAW

## The INGREDIENTS I need

| | |
|---|---|
| 1 small head | Green Cabbage, shredded |
| 1 small | Carrot, grated |
| 1/2 cup | Salad Dressing |
| 2 Tbsp. | Sugar |
| 1/8 tsp. | Salt |
| 2 Tbsp. | Vinegar |

## The EQUIPMENT I need

Bowl
Grater
Measuring cup/spoons

## ᗷᗷᗷᗷᗷᗷᗷᗷᗷᗷᗷᗷᗷᗷᗷᗷ How To Make It ᗷᗷᗷᗷᗷᗷᗷᗷᗷᗷᗷᗷᗷᗷᗷᗷ

1. Wash cabbage and carrot.
2. Shred cabbage and grate carrot.
3. Add salad dressing, sugar, salt and vinegar.
4. Mix well in bowl.
5. Chill.

**Serves 4-5**

# CRANBERRY MOLD

## The INGREDIENTS I need

| | |
|---|---|
| 1 pkg. | Gelatin |
| 1 cup + 3 T. | Water |
| 1 pkg. | Lemon Jello |
| 1 16-oz. can | Whole Cranberry Sauce |
| Rind | from 1 Orange, grated |
| Juice | from 1 Orange |
| 3-1/2 T. | Lemon Juice |

## The EQUIPMENT I need

Pot
Measuring cup/spoon
Wooden spoon
Can Opener
Grater
Mold pan

ꝏꝏꝏꝏꝏꝏꝏꝏꝏꝏ **How To Make It** ꝏꝏꝏꝏꝏꝏꝏꝏꝏꝏ

1. Soften gelatin in 3 tablespoons of cold water.
2. Boil 1 cup water and dissolve lemon jello.
3. Mix in softened gelatin.
4. Add all other ingredients and mix well.
5. Pour in mold pan and chill overnight.

**Serves 6**

# CUCUMBER SALAD

## The INGREDIENTS I need

| | |
|---|---|
| 2 medium | Cucumbers |
| 1/2 Tbsp. | Sugar |
| 1/3 cup | White Vinegar |
| 1 small | Onion, sliced |
| 1/2 tsp. | Salt |
| 1/8 tsp. | Pepper |

## The EQUIPMENT I need

Bowl
Cutting board/knife
Measuring cup/spoons

8888888888888888 **How To Make It** 8888888888888888

1. Peel cucumbers and onion.
2. Slice very thin.
3. Put them in a small bowl and sprinkle with salt.
4. Put in refrigerator for 30 minutes.
5. Mix vinegar, sugar and pepper until the sugar dissolves.
6. Add to the cucumbers. Serve very cold.

**Serves 3-4**

# DEVILED EGGS

## The INGREDIENTS I need

| | |
|---|---|
| 6 | Eggs, hard-boiled |
| 2 T. | Mayonnaise or Salad Dressing |
| 1-1/2 tsp. | Prepared Mustard |
| 1-1/2 tsp. | Vinegar |
| 3 T. | Sweet Pickle Relish |

Salt and Pepper to taste
Paprika

## The EQUIPMENT I need

Small bowl
Measuring spoons
Fork
Knife
Spoon

8888888888888888 **How To Make It** 8888888888888888

1. Peel hard-cooked eggs and cut down center.
2. Remove yolks and mash with fork.
3. Add mayonnaise, mustard, vinegar and relish until mixture forms a smooth paste.
4. Add salt and pepper to taste.
5. Fill egg whites with yolk mixture.
6. Top with paprika.
7. Refrigerate for one hour before serving.

**Serves 4**

# MACARONI SALAD

## The INGREDIENTS I need

| | |
|---|---|
| 2 cups | Elbow Macaroni |
| 1/2 cup | Salad Dressing |
| 1/4 cup | Sweet Pickle Relish |
| 1/4 cup | Pimentos, chopped |
| 1/2 tsp. | Sugar |
| 1/2 tsp. | Salt |
| 1/4 cup | Bell Pepper, chopped |
| 1/4 cup | Onions, chopped |

## The EQUIPMENT I need

Pot
Measuring cup/spoons
Bowl
Spoon
Cutting board
Knife
Colander

## 8888888888888888 How To Make It 8888888888888888

1. Boil macaroni for 20 minutes
2. Drain
3. Add macaroni, salad dressing, relish in bowl together.
4. Chop pimentos, bell pepper and onions.
5. Mix together sugar and salt.
6. Refrigerate and chill.

**Serves 3-4**

# POTATO SALAD

## The INGREDIENTS I need

| | |
|---|---|
| 3 cups | Potatoes, diced or cubed cooked |
| 2 | Eggs, chopped, hard-cooked |
| 1/2 cup | Celery, chopped |
| 1/2 cup | Onions, diced |
| 1/4 cup | Sweet Pickle Relish |
| 1/2 tsp. | Salt |
| 1 tsp. | Vinegar |
| 1/2 tsp. | Pepper |
| 1 cup | Mayonnaise or Salad Dressing |
| 1/4 tsp. | Celery Seed, (optional) |

## The EQUIPMENT I need

Pot
Bowl
Measuring cup/spoons
Cutting board/knife
Large spoon

## ꙮꙮꙮꙮꙮꙮꙮꙮꙮ How To Make It ꙮꙮꙮꙮꙮꙮꙮꙮꙮ

1. Cover potatoes with water; bring to boil.
2. Lower flame and simmer until tender.
3. Drain, peel and cut into small bite-sized pieces.
4. Add chopped onions, celery and eggs to potatoes and mix with the remaining ingredients.
5. Cover bowl and refrigerate about 2 hours.

Serves 4-6

# TOMATO AND ONION VINAGRETTE

## The INGREDIENTS I need

| | |
|---|---|
| 2 medium | Tomatoes, thinly sliced |
| 1 medium | Red or Yellow Onion, thinly sliced |
| 1 Tbsp. | Vegetable Oil |
| 1 tsp. | Red Wine Vinegar |
| 1/4 tsp. | Sugar |
| 1/4 tsp. | Oregano Leaves |
| 1/4 tsp. | Salt |
| 1/4 tsp. | Pepper |
| 1/8 tsp. | Chopped Parsley, (optional) |

## The EQUIPMENT I need

Serving dishes
Measuring cup/spoons
Cutting board/knife
Foil
Jar

ꝸꝸꝸꝸꝸꝸꝸꝸꝸꝸꝸꝸꝸꝸꝸꝸ **How To Make It** ꝸꝸꝸꝸꝸꝸꝸꝸꝸꝸꝸꝸꝸꝸꝸꝸ

1. Arrange tomatoes and onions on serving dish, overlapping slices.
2. Combine all ingredients; shake thoroughly to blend.
3. Sprinkle over tomatoes and onions.
4. Cover and refrigerate until serving time.
5. Garnish with parsley.

Serves 3-4

# TOSSED GREEN SALAD

## The INGREDIENTS I need

| | |
|---|---|
| 1 head | Lettuce (Iceberg, Romaine or Spinach) |
| 2 | Celery Stalks, sliced |
| 2 | Tomatoes, cut into quarters |
| 1/2 small | Cucumber, sliced thin |
| 1 | Carrot, sliced or grated |
| 4 | Radishes, cut into quarters |
| 1/2 cup | Croutons, (optional) |

## The EQUIPMENT I need

Knife/cutting board
Paper towels or
Salad spinner
Salad bowl

## ꙮꙮꙮꙮꙮꙮꙮꙮꙮꙮꙮ How To Make It ꙮꙮꙮꙮꙮꙮꙮꙮꙮꙮꙮ

1. Wash and dry all the vegetables before you cut them up.
2. Wash and dry the salad greens very thoroughly and carefully.
3. Use paper towels or a salad spinner if you have one.
4. Always dry the lettuce thoroughly, Damp leaves will make a wilted (limp or soft) salad instead of a crispy, crunchy one.
5. Tear the lettuce into small pieces with your fingers.
6. Put all the ingredients (except croutons) into the salad bowl.
7. Toss it with your favorite dressing.
8. Sprinkle the croutons on top.

Serves 3-4

# VEGETABLES

## *Little Green Acres*

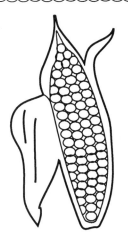

Corn on the Cob
Fried Corn
Succotash

Okra, Corn & Tomatoes
Okra & Tomatoes
Fried Green Tomatoes

Fried Okra

String Beans

Peas & Carrots

**Greens**
Collard
Kale
Mustard
Smothered Cabbage
Turnip
Mashed Turnips

# STRING BEANS

## The INGREDIENTS I need

| | |
|---|---|
| 1 pound | String beans, fresh (or 2 pkg. frozen) |
| 2 pieces | Salt pork, small or smoked turkey pieces |
| 4 cups | Water |
| Salt | To taste |
| 1 medium | Onion, sliced |

## The EQUIPMENT I need

Pot/lid
Measuring cup/spoons
Knife/cutting board

ꝋꝋꝋꝋꝋꝋꝋꝋꝋꝋꝋꝋꝋꝋꝋ **How To Make It** ꝋꝋꝋꝋꝋꝋꝋꝋꝋꝋꝋꝋꝋꝋꝋ

1. Cook salt pork or turkey in a pot for 1 hour.
2. Wash beans and cut off tips (snapped).
3. Add beans, salt and onions to water.
4. Cook covered for 30 minutes.

**Serves 4**

# CORN ON THE COB

## The INGREDIENTS I need

| | |
|---|---|
| 2 ears | Corn |
| 2 cups | Boiling Water |
| 1 tsp. | Salt |
| 2 Tbsp. | Butter |

## The EQUIPMENT I need

Pot
Measuring cup/spoons
Fork
Knife

### &&&&&&&&&&&&&&&&& How To Make It &&&&&&&&&&&&&&&&&

1. Place corn in boiling water.
2. Add salt.
3. Boil corn for 30 minutes.
4. Remove corn, add butter and salt to taste.

Serves 2

# FRIED CORN

## The INGREDIENTS I need

6 Ears    Corn, fresh shucked
1/4 cup   Bacon Fat or
          Vegetable Oil
2 Tbsp.   Flour
1 Tbsp.   Sugar
1 tsp.    Pepper

## The EQUIPMENT I need

Cutting board/knife
Measuring cup/spoons
Skillet
Bowl
Wooden spoon

8888888888888888 **How To Make It** 888888888888888

1. Cut the grains formt he ears of corn with knife.
2. Scrape the cobs to get all the milky liquid.
3. In a bowl, mix the corn, flour, sugar and pepper.
4. Pour the corn mixture into skillet with the oil.
5. Stir fry until done; cook about 20 minutes.

Note: If you can't get fresh corn, you can substitute 1 can of cream-style corn and 1 can of whole kernel corn.

Serves 3-4

# SUCCOTASH

## The INGREDIENTS I need

| | |
|---|---|
| 1 cup | Corn, (canned or frozen) cooked |
| 1 cup | Lima Beans, (canned or frozen) cooked |
| 1/2 tsp. | Salt |
| 2 Tbsp. | Margarine |
| Dash | Pepper |

## The EQUIPMENT I need

Pot
Can opener
Measuring cup/spoons

## 8888888888888888 How To Make It 8888888888888888

1. Combine corn and lima beans in pot.
2. Add salt, pepper and margarine.
3. Heat slowly over low heat for 10 minutes.

Serves 4

# COLLARD GREENS

## The INGREDIENTS I need

3-4 Bunches Collard Greens
2 cups Water
1 Ham Hock or Salt Pork (small piece)
1 Tbsp. Sugar
1 tsp. Salt
1/2 tsp. Pepper

## The EQUIPMENT I need

Large Pot
Measuring cup/spoons

## ᪣᪣᪣᪣᪣᪣᪣᪣᪣᪣᪣᪣᪣ How To Make It ᪣᪣᪣᪣᪣᪣᪣᪣᪣᪣᪣᪣᪣

1. Wash and remove stems from greens.
2. Boil ham hock or salt pork for 1 hour in water.
3. Tear leaves into bite-sized pieces.
4. Add greens, sugar, salt and pepper.
5. Cover and cook greens slowly until tender.
6. Simmer for 2 hours.

Serves 4

# KALE GREENS

## The INGREDIENTS I need

## The EQUIPMENT I need

| | | |
|---|---|---|
| 3 quarts | Water | Pot/lid |
| 3 pounds | Kale | Measuring spoons |
| 1/4 pound | Seasoning Meat, (Fat Back, lean Salt Pork, Ham or Smoked Turkey pieces) | Knife |
| 1 tsp. | Sugar | |
| 1 tsp. | Crushed Red Pepper | |

Salt and Pepper to taste

## ꝏꝏꝏꝏꝏꝏꝏꝏꝏꝏꝏꝏꝏꝏ How To Make It ꝏꝏꝏꝏꝏꝏꝏꝏꝏꝏꝏꝏꝏꝏ

1. Place the meat in the water with the red pepper.
2. Cook with lid on for about 1-1/2 hours or until meat is tender.
3. Wash kale several times.
4. Remove sand and dirt.
5. Trim off the root and heavier part of the leaf.
6. Remove meat and put the kale in a cook until tender.
7. Replace the meat on top and heat thoroughly.

Serves 4-6

# MUSTARD GREENS

## The INGREDIENTS I need

| | |
|---|---|
| 2-3 bunches | Mustard Greens |
| 1/4 pound | Salt Pork, |
| | Ham Hock, |
| | Neckbone, or |
| | Smoked Turkey pieces |
| 2 cups | Water |
| 1 Tbsp. | Sugar |

Salt and Pepper to taste

## The EQUIPMENT I need

Pot/lid
Measuring cup/spoons

〰〰〰〰〰〰〰〰〰〰〰 **How To Make It** 〰〰〰〰〰〰〰〰〰〰〰

1. Wash greens thoroughly.
2. Put greens in pot and add water.
3. Add meat and seasoning.
4. Cover and cook on low heat for 40 minutes or until meat and greens are tender.
5. Add salt and sugar; cook another 15 minutes.

Serves 4-6

# SMOTHERED CABBAGE

## The INGREDIENTS I need

| | |
|---|---|
| 1 3-4 pound | Head of Cabbage |
| 1/2 cup | Bacon Fat |
| 1 large | Onion, chopped |
| 1 tsp. | Salt |
| 1/2 tsp. | Black Pepper |

## The EQUIPMENT I need

Frying pan/lid
Measuring cup/spoons
Cutting board/knife

## How To Make It

1. Wash the cabbage.
2. Chop into small pieces.
3. Melt the bacon fat in frying pan with a cover.
4. Add vegetables and seasonings.
5. Cover and cook over low heat for 1 hour.
6. Stir to prevent sticking to the pan.

**Serves 4-6**

# TURNIP GREENS

## The INGREDIENTS I need

3 pounds    Turnip Greens
1 pound    Turnips, peeled
           (optional)
1 quart    Water
1/4 pound    Seasoning Meat
           (Fatback, Lean Salt Pork,
           Ham Hock or Smoked
           Turkey pieces)
1/2 tsp.    Salt
1/4 tsp.    Pepper

## The EQUIPMENT I need

Large pot/lid
Measuring cup/spoons
Cutting board/knife

## 8888888888888888 How To Make It 88888888888888

1. Wash greens thoroughly several times.
2. Throw away any yellow leaves or heavy stems.
3. Cook meat covered with water (about 20 minutes) until it boils.
4. Cut the greens into small pieces.
6. Add greens and bring to hard boil.
7. Cover and lower heat and cook slowly for 2 hours or until tender.
8. Add peeled and diced turnips on top of greens for 20 minutes.

Serves 4-6

# MASHED TURNIPS

## The INGREDIENTS I need

1 pound  White Turnips
1/2 tsp.  Salt
1/4 tsp.  Sugar
1-1/2  T.  Butter,
　　　　　Margarine or Bacon Fat

## The EQUIPMENT I need

Potato Peeler
Knife/cutting board
Measuring spoons
Pot/lid
Colander
Fork

## 88888888888888 How To Make It 8888888888888

1. Peel and quarter the turnips.
2. Place them in a pot and cover them with water.
3. Add salt.
4. Simmer for 20 minutes or until turnips are fork tender; drain.
5. Mash and add sugar and butter.

**Serves 4**

# FRIED OKRA

## The INGREDIENTS I need

| | |
|---|---|
| 8 pods | Okra |
| 1 cup | Yellow Cornmeal |
| 1 Tbsp. | Flour |
| 1 tsp. | Salt |
| 1/2 tsp. | Pepper |
| 1/4 cup | Vegetable Oil |

## The EQUIPMENT I need

Knife/cutting board
Measuring cup/spoons
Skillet
Paper towel
Spoon/tongs

## How To Make It

1. Slice okra into 1/4-inch slices.
2. Wash okra in cold water.
3. Mix cornmeal, flour salt and pepper together.
4. Roll okra in cornmeal mix.
5. Fry in hot skillet for 10 minutes until golden brown.
6. Drain on paper towel.

**Serves 6**

# OKRA, CORN AND TOMATOES

## The INGREDIENTS I need

| | |
|---|---|
| 2 cans | Whole Fresh Corn, or 4 Fresh Corn |
| 1 pkg. | Frozen Okra, or fresh (cut up) |
| 1 | Bell Pepper |
| 1 | Onion, chopped |
| 1 /2 cup | Vegetable Oil |
| 1/2 tsp. | Sugar |
| 1/2 tsp. | Salt |
| 1 can | Tomatoes or 2 Fresh Tomatoes |

## The EQUIPMENT I need

Can opener
Knife/cutting board
Measuring cup/spoon
Skillet
Wooden spoon

## ৪৪৪৪৪৪৪৪৪৪৪৪৪৪ How To Make It ৪৪৪৪৪৪৪৪৪৪৪৪৪৪

1. Slightly brown onions, okra and bell pepper.
2. Keep stirring; add corn and tomatoes.
3. Cook for 10 minutes or until fresh corn is tender.

Serves 6

# OKRA AND TOMATOES

## The INGREDIENTS I need

| | |
|---|---|
| 2 cups | Okra, (fresh or frozen)* |
| 1 can | Stewed Tomatoes or 2 cups Tomatoes |
| 1 small | Onion, chopped |
| 1/4 pound | Smoked Sweet Sausage or Smoked Turkey Pieces, (optional) |

Salt and Pepper to taste

## The EQUIPMENT I need

Skillet
Pot/lid
Measuring cup
Cutting board/knife

ᦸᦸᦸᦸᦸᦸᦸᦸᦸᦸᦸᦸᦸᦸᦸ **How To Make It** ᦸᦸᦸᦸᦸᦸᦸᦸᦸᦸᦸᦸᦸᦸᦸ

1. Fry meat, (optional).
2. Place other ingredients in a saucepan.
3. When meat is done add to the vegetables.
4. Cover the pot.
5. Simmer over low heat for 25 minutes.
6. Add no water. The liquid from the canned tomatoes should be enough.

*If frozen okra is used, cook tomatoes and onions for 15 minutes before adding okra to the pot.

**Serves 4**

 - - - - - - - - - - - - - - - - - - - - - - - - - - - - - - *LITTLE GREEN ACRES*

# PEAS AND CARROTS

## The INGREDIENTS I need

| | |
|---|---|
| 2 T. | Butter or Margarine |
| 1 16-oz. can | Green Peas, drained or frozen |
| 2 | Carrots, diced |
| 1tsp. | Sugar (Optional) |

Salt and Pepper to taste

## The EQUIPMENT I need

Pot/lid
Can opener
Measuring spoon
Knife/cutting board

## ✋✋✋✋✋✋✋✋✋✋ How To Make It ✋✋✋✋✋✋✋✋✋✋

1. Cut carrots and cook for 10 minutes.
2. Add peas and margarine.
3. Add sugar, salt and pepper.
4. Cover and reduce heat.
5. Cook for 5 minutes or until heated thoroughly.

Serves 4

# FRIED GREEN TOMATOES

## The INGREDIENTS I need

| | |
|---|---|
| 2 | Tomatoes, green |
| 1 cup | Cornmeal |
| 1 tsp. | Salt |
| 1 tsp. | Pepper |
| 1 Tbsp. | Flour |
| 1 cup | Oil |

## The EQUIPMENT I need

Knife
Measuring cup/spoons
Skillet
Bowl

### ꝸꝸꝸꝸꝸꝸꝸꝸꝸꝸꝸꝸꝸꝸꝸꝸꝸ How To Make It ꝸꝸꝸꝸꝸꝸꝸꝸꝸꝸꝸꝸꝸꝸꝸꝸꝸ

1. Slice tomatoes into 1/2 inch slices.
2. Mix cornmeal, salt, pepper and flour together.
3. Dip tomatoes in meal mixture.
4. Cover on both sides.
5. Fry each side to golden brown.

Serves 2

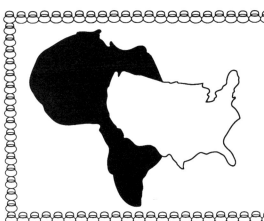

# MEATS

## *From the Smokehouse*

Barbecue Meats

Country Fried Steak

Liver and Onions

Meatloaf

Oxtail

Pot Roast

Roast Beef

Roast Leg of Lamb

Short Ribs of Beef

# BARBECUE MEATS

## The INGREDIENTS I need

### The EQUIPMENT I need

For Juneteenth • 4th of July • Family Reunions

Hamburger
Hot Dogs
Hot Links
Steak
Marinade Sauce, Bottle
 OR
Barbecue Sauce, Bottle

Tongs
Fork
Spatula
Basting brush
Pot holders
Spray-basting bottle
Charcoal briquets
Charcoal lighter fluid
Matches
Grill or Pit

ᎧᎧᎧᎧᎧᎧᎧᎧᎧᎧᎧᎧᎧᎧᎧᎧᎧ **How To Make It** ᎧᎧᎧᎧᎧᎧᎧᎧᎧᎧᎧᎧᎧᎧᎧᎧᎧ

Hamburgers:   Brown 3 to 5 minutes on each side.

Hot Dogs:   Turn frequently 3 to 5 minutes.  Place buns split side down around edge of grill until lightly toasted or softly warm.  Serve with condiments desired.

Hot Links:   Turn several times for 10 to 12 minutes.

Steaks:   Baste and turn every three minutes for 10 minutes for rare meat or Cook and baste until done the way you like it.

# COUNTRY FRIED STEAK

## The INGREDIENTS I need

| | |
|---|---|
| 1 - 1-1/2 pound | Round Steak, cubed |
| 2 Tbsp. | Flour |
| 2 cups | Water, hot |
| 1 pkg. | Lipton's French Onion Soup |
| 1 Tbsp. | Oil |

Salt and Pepper to taste

## The EQUIPMENT I need

Iron skillet/lid
Bowl
Measuring cup/spoons
Wooden spoon
Fork

## How To Make It

1. Combine the onion soup and hot water in bowl.
2. Brown the steak in the oil on both sides.
3. Remove the steak from skillet.
4. Add 2 Tbsp. of flour and stir.
5. Add the onion soup mix.
6. Salt and pepper to taste.
7. Put the steak back into the skillet.
8. Cover and simmer for 1 hour, stirring occasionally.

**Serves 6**

# LIVER AND ONIONS

## The INGREDIENTS I need

1 pound    Beef Liver
            Salt and Pepper to taste
1/2 cup    Flour
1/2 cup    Water
1           Onion, sliced
2 Tbsp.    Bacon Fat or Vegetable Oil

## The EQUIPMENT I need

Knife/cutting board
Measuring cup/spoons
Skillet
Wooden spoon1 Onion, sliced

## ଓଓଓଓଓଓଓଓଓଓଓଓଓ How To Make It ଓଓଓଓଓଓଓଓଓଓଓଓଓ

1. Season liver with salt and pepper.
2. Roll in flour.
3. Heat the bacon fat or vegetable oil in skillet.
4. Fry until golden brown on both sides.
5. Remove liver from skillet.
6. Brown onions in the fat.
7. Return liver to skillet and add water gradually.
8. Stir constantly for 5 minutes.

**Serves 5**

# MEAT LOAF

## The INGREDIENTS I need

1-1/2 Pounds Ground Beef
1 small      Onion, chopped
1/2 cup      Green Pepper, chopped
1 slice      White Bread, crumbled
1      Egg, beaten
1 cup      Milk
1 tsp.      Salt
1/4 tsp.      Pepper
1/2 cup      Carrots, mashed and cooked
1/4 cup      Tomato Paste
1/4 tsp.      Sugar

## The EQUIPMENT I need

Cutting board/knife
Measuring cup/spoons
Bowl
Loaf pan

## ଼଼଼଼଼଼଼଼଼଼଼଼଼଼ How To Make It ଼଼଼଼଼଼଼଼଼଼଼଼଼଼

1. Preheat oven to 350 degrees.
2. Chop onions and green peppers.
3. Mix together all ingredients in bowl and mix well.
4. Shape into meat loaf.
5. Place in a greased loaf pan.
6. Bake uncovered for one hour.

Serves 4-6

# OXTAIL

## The INGREDIENTS I need

| | |
|---|---|
| 2 pounds | Oxtails |
| 3 Tbsp. | Oil |
| 1 cup | Tomato Sauce |
| 1 cup | Hot Water |
| 1 large | Onion, chopped |
| 1 clove | Garlic |
| 1 | Bay Leaf |
| 1/2 tsp. | Salt |
| 1/4 tsp. | Pepper |
| 1 Tbsp. | Lemon Juice or Vinegar |
| 1 Tbsp. | Sugar |
| 1/2 cup | Flour |

## The EQUIPMENT I need

Pot/lid
Measuring cup/spoons
Cutting board/knife
Wooden spoon

## 8888888888888888 How To Make It 8888888888888888

1. Roll the oxtail pieces in flour which has been seasoned with salt and pepper.
2. Brown on all sides in hot oil.
3. Add the remaining ingredients.
4. Cover and simmer gently until the meat is tender about 3 to 4 hours.
5. Use remaining seasoned flour to thicken liquid for gravy.

**Serves 4**

# POT ROAST

## The INGREDIENTS I need

| | |
|---|---|
| 3-4 pounds | Chuck Roast |
| 2 Tbsp. | Oil |
| 1 tsp. | Salt |
| 1/4 tsp. | Pepper |
| 2 Tbsp. | Flour |
| 1 cup | Celery, diced |
| 1 cup | Carrots, diced |
| 4 | Potatoes, diced |
| 1 | Bay Leaf |
| 1 small can | Tomato Sauce |
| 2 cups | Water |

## The EQUIPMENT I need

Pot/lid
Measuring cup/spoons
Cutting board/knife
Wooden spoon
Platter

## ꙮꙮꙮꙮꙮꙮꙮꙮ How To Make It ꙮꙮꙮꙮꙮꙮꙮꙮ

1. Sprinkle meat with salt, pepper and flour and brown in oil on all sides in pot.
2. Add water, tomato sauce and bay leaf. Cover and simmer for two hours.
3. Add onion, celery, carrot and potatoes to pot.
4. Cover, simmer for one hour.
5. Put meat on a platter.
6. Place vegetables around meat.

**Serves 6-8**

# ROAST BEEF

## The INGREDIENTS I need

| | |
|---|---|
| 1 | Standing Rib Roast (3 ribs) |
| | Salt |
| | Pepper |

## The EQUIPMENT I need

Roasting pan

8888888888888888 **How To Make It** 88888888888888888

1. Heat oven to 450-500 degrees, very hot.
2. Wash meat.
3. Season with salt and pepper.
4. Place in roasting pan fat side up.
5. Cook in a hot oven for 18 to 20 minutes per pound. After 20 minutes, turn heat down to 300 degrees for the rest of the cooking time.

**Serves 8-10**

# ROAST LEG OF LAMB

## The INGREDIENTS I need

| | |
|---|---|
| 1 | Leg of Lamb |
| 1/3 cup | Vinegar |
| 1/2 tsp. | Garlic Powder |
| 2 medium | Onions |

Salt and Pepper to taste

## The EQUIPMENT I need

Paper towel
Knife/cutting board
Foil
Roasting pan

## 888888888888888 How To Make It 888888888888888

1. Wash the lamb.
2. Pat dry and then pat well with vinegar.
3. Season with salt, pepper and garlic powder.
4. Cut onions into slices and lay under the lamb.
5. Leave in the refrigerator several hours or overnight.
6. Bake in a covered pan with a little water in it.
7. Start at 400 degrees and bake for one hour.
8. Reduce the heat to 325 degrees and finish baking for 1-1/2 hours or until tender.
9. Use the juices for a gravy or mint sauce.

Serves 8-10

# SHORT RIBS OF BEEF

## The INGREDIENTS I need

3 pounds    Short Ribs or Beef
2 Tbsp.     Oil
3 Tbsp.     Flour
2 large     Onions, chopped
2           Celery Stalks, chopped
4 cups      Water

Salt and Pepper to taste

## The EQUIPMENT I need

Pot/lid
Measuring cup/spoons
Cutting board/knife

## ᵟᵟᵟᵟᵟᵟᵟᵟᵟᵟᵟᵟᵟᵟᵟᵟ How To Make It ᵟᵟᵟᵟᵟᵟᵟᵟᵟᵟᵟᵟᵟᵟᵟᵟ

1. Season short ribs with salt and pepper. Dredge with flour.
2. Brown the ribs in the oil.
3. Brown onions.
4. Add celery and water to the pan.
5. Cover. Bring to a boil. Lower heat.
6. Simmer 2-1/2 to 3 hours. Stir occasionally.

**Serves 4-6**

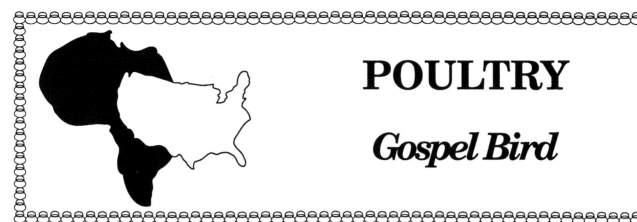

# POULTRY
## *Gospel Bird*

Baked Chicken

Chicken and Dumplings

(Dumpling Batter)

Chicken Pot Pie

Oven-Baked
Barbecued Chicken
Smothered Chicken

Southern Fried Chicken

Stewed Chicken

Roast Turkey
Bread Stuffing

Cornbread Stuffing

# BAKED CHICKEN

## The INGREDIENTS I need

3 pounds    Chicken, cut
into pieces
Salt to taste
1/2 tsp.    Garlic Powder
4 Tbsp.    Margarine, melted

## The EQUIPMENT I need

Pan for baking
Measuring spoons
Brush

8888888888888888 **How To Make It** 8888888888888888

1. Preheat oven to 400 degrees.
2. Wash the chicken in cold water and pat dry.
3. Season with salt and garlic powder.
4. Place in a shallow baking pan.
5. Brush with melted margarine.
6. Roast uncovered at 400 degrees until the chicken begins to brown, 10-15 minutes.
7. Lower the heat to 325 degrees. Bake for 40 minutes.

**Serves 4**

# CHICKEN AND DUMPLINGS

## The INGREDIENTS I need

| | |
|---|---|
| 3-4 pounds | Chicken, cut up |
| 1 tsp. | Salt |
| 1/2 tsp. | Pepper |
| 1 cup | Onions, chopped |
| 1 cup | Carrots, chopped |
| 1 cup | Celery, chopped |
| 1 | Green Pepper, diced |
| 2 Tbsp. | Parsley, chopped |
| 1 | Bay Leaf |
| 6 cups | Water |
| 6 Tbsp. | Bacon Fat, Butter or Margarine |

## The EQUIPMENT I need

Skillet
Large pot/cover
Cutting board/knife
Measuring cup/spoons
Wooden spoon

### ଌଌଌଌଌଌଌଌଌଌଌଌଌଌଌ How To Make It ଌଌଌଌଌଌଌଌଌଌଌଌଌଌଌ

1. Wash meat and dry. Season with salt and pepper. Dredge with flour.
2. In a frying pan, saute remaining ingredients. Brown chicken in it.
3. Pour chicken, onions, green pepper, celery, carrots, bay leaf and water into a large pot.
4. Bring to a boil. Lower heat. Cover and simmer for 30 minutes.
5. Meanwhile, to make the dumpling batter, sift the flour, baking powder and salt together in a bowl.*
6. Add egg, milk and melted margarine.
7. Drop dumpling batter by the tablespoonfuls into the pot.
8. Cover pot and simmer 20 minutes.

**Serves 4-6**

*See Dumpling Batter Recipe on the next page

# DUMPLING BATTER

## The INGREDIENTS I need

| | |
|---|---|
| 1-1/4 cups | Flour |
| 1-1/2 tsp. | Baking Powder |
| 1 tsp. | Salt |
| 1 | Egg, beaten |
| 1/2 cup | Milk |
| 1 Tbsp. | Butter or Margarine, melted |

## The EQUIPMENT I need

Bowl
Measuring cup/spoons
Sifter

ꝸꝸꝸꝸꝸꝸꝸꝸꝸꝸꝸꝸꝸꝸꝸꝸ **How To Make It** ꝸꝸꝸꝸꝸꝸꝸꝸꝸꝸꝸꝸꝸꝸꝸꝸ

See CHICKEN AND DUMPLINGS Recipe on the previous page

# CHICKEN POT PIE

## The INGREDIENTS I need

| | |
|---|---|
| 4-5 pounds | Stewing Chicken, cut up |
| 1 medium | Onion, chopped |
| 1 cup | Peas, cooked |
| 1 cup | Carrots, cooked |
| 3 Tbsp. | Flour |
| 4 Tbsp. | Chicken Fat |
| 1 cup | Chicken Broth |
| 1 cup | Milk |
| 2 tsp. | Salt |
| 1 tsp. | Pepper |

## The EQUIPMENT I need

Pot/lid
Casserole pan
Measuring cup/spoons
Cutting board/knife
Wooden spoon
Whisk

8888888888888888 **How To Make It** 8888888888888888

1. Place cut up chicken pieces in pot of water to cover and bring to boil.
2. Add onions, carrots, peas, salt and pepper.
3. Cover and simmer until chicken is tender.
4. Remove bones from chicken but leave the meat in large pieces.
5. Make a gravy using 4 Tbsp. chicken fat, flour, chicken broth and milk.
6. Place chicken in a casserole and pour the hot gravy over it.
7. Cover with a baking powder biscuit dough.
8. Make a few slashes in the dough.
9. Bake at 450 degrees until dough is browned about 15 to 20 minutes.

Serves 6

# OVEN BAKED BARBECUED CHICKEN

## The INGREDIENTS I need

| | |
|---|---|
| 3 pounds | Chicken, cut into pieces |
| 1 tsp. | Salt |
| 1/2 tsp. | Onion Salt |
| 4 tsp. | Worcestershire |
| 4 drops | Tabasco |
| 1/4 pound | Butter or Margarine, melted |
| 4 Tbsp. | Vinegar |
| 1/3 cup | Water |

## The EQUIPMENT I need

Roasting pan
Measuring cup/spoons
Cutting board/knife
Brush for basting

## 88888888888888 How To Make It 88888888888888

1. Set oven at 375 degrees.
2. Season meat with salt and onion salt.
3. Place chicken in a roasting pan.
4. Combine the remaining ingredients and brush the meat with the sauce.
5. Bake uncovered in the oven for 30 minutes.
6. Add small amounts of water if sauce sticks to the pan.

Serves 4

# SMOTHERED CHICKEN

## The INGREDIENTS I need

| | |
|---|---|
| 3 pounds | Chicken |
| 1/4 tsp. | Salt |
| 1/4 tsp. | Pepper |
| Dash | Paprika |
| 1/4 cup | Flour |
| 4 Tbsp. | Butter or Margarine |
| 2 Tbsp. | Onion, minced, |
| 2 Cubes | Chicken Bouillon |
| 2 cups | Water, hot |
| 3 Tbsp. | Green Pepper, chopped |

## The EQUIPMENT I need

Pot/lid
Measuring cup/spoons
Cutting board/knife

## ୫୫୫୫୫୫୫୫୫୫୫୫୫ How To Make It ୫୫୫୫୫୫୫୫୫୫୫୫୫

1. Wash chicken in cold water.
2. Pat dry.  Season with salt, pepper and paprika.
3. Dredge with flour.
4. Brown chicken on all sides in butter or margarine.
5. Add onions and brown.
6. Stir in bouillon or water. Add green peppers.
7. Cover pot.  Simmer for 1 hour or until meat is tender.

Serves 4

# SOUTHERN FRIED CHICKEN

## The INGREDIENTS I need

4 pieces Chicken
1/2 cup Flour
1/8 tsp. Salt
1/8 tsp. Pepper
2 cups Oil (for frying)

## The EQUIPMENT I need

Frying pan
Measuring cup/spoons
Brown lunch bag or
plastic bag

## How To Make It

1. Wash chicken pieces.
2. Mix flour, salt and pepper together.
3. Put chicken in bag and shake until covered.
4. Drop chicken in hot oil.
5. Fry until golden brown for 20 minutes.
6. Drain on paper towels.

Serves 4

# STEWED CHICKEN

## The INGREDIENTS I need

| | |
|---|---|
| 3 pounds | Chicken cut into pieces |
| 2 medium | Onions, minced |
| 1 stalk | Celery, minced |
| 1 large | Green Pepper, diced |
| 2-1/2 cups | Stewed Tomatoes, canned |
| 1 tsp. | Salt |
| 1/4 tsp. | Black Pepper |
| 2 cups | Water |

## The EQUIPMENT I need

Large pot/lid
Measuring cup/spoons
Cutting board/knife
Can opener

## ☺☺☺☺☺☺☺☺☺☺☺☺☺☺ How To Make It ☺☺☺☺☺☺☺☺☺☺☺☺☺

1. Place all of the ingredients in a large pot.
2. Bring to a boil (10 minutes).
3. Cover and simmer for 1 hour.

Serves 4-6

# ROAST TURKEY

## The INGREDIENTS I need

10-12 pound Turkey
2 Tbsp.     Butter or Margarine
1/2 cup     Water

## The EQUIPMENT I need

Roasting pan
Pastry brush
Measuring cup/spoons
Turkey lacer
Foil

ꝏꝏꝏꝏꝏꝏꝏꝏꝏꝏꝏ **How To Make It** ꝏꝏꝏꝏꝏꝏꝏꝏꝏꝏꝏ

1. Wash and pat turkey dry.
2. Place dressing in neck cavity.
3. Allow 1 cup stuffing per pound.
4. Secure with turkey lacers.
5. Brush entire bird with melted margarine.
6. Place the turkey breast side up in roasting pan.
7. Allow 30 minutes cooking time per pound. Roast at 325 degrees, i.e. 8 lb. turkey roasts in 4 hours.
8. Baste with butter or margarine during roasting period.
9. Cover loosely with foil to prevent over browning.

**Serves 10-12**

# BREAD STUFFING

## The INGREDIENTS I need

| | |
|---|---|
| 1/2 cup | Butter or Margarine |
| 1 cup | Celery, chopped |
| 1 cup | Onion, chopped |
| 1/2 tsp. | Sage |
| 1/2 tsp. | Poultry Seasoning |
| 1/2 tsp. | Salt |
| 1/4 tsp. | Black Pepper |
| 4 cups | White Bread, crumbled dry or |
| | Crumb Stuffing Mix |

## The EQUIPMENT I need

Frying Pan
Measuring cup/spoons
Wooden spoon

ꙮꙮꙮꙮꙮꙮꙮꙮꙮꙮꙮꙮꙮ **How To Make It** ꙮꙮꙮꙮꙮꙮꙮꙮꙮꙮꙮꙮꙮ

1. Melt the butter or margarine in a frying pan.
2. Saute onion; add remaining ingredients.
3. Stir until all ingredients are well blended.

**Makes 3 cups**

# CORNBREAD STUFFING

## The INGREDIENTS I need

| | |
|---|---|
| 1/2 cup | Butter or Margarine |
| 1 cup | Celery, chopped |
| 1 cup | Onion, chopped |
| 1 | Egg, well beaten |
| 1 cup | Giblet Broth or Chicken Stock |
| 1 tsp. | Poultry Seasoning |
| 2 Tbsp. | Parsley |
| 1 tsp. | Sage |
| 1 tsp. | Salt |
| 1 tsp. | Black Pepper |
| 1/2 tsp. | Thyme |
| 4 cups | Cornbread Stuffing Crumbs |

## The EQUIPMENT I need

Frying pan
Baking pan
Measuring cup/spoons
Cutting board/knife
Mixing bowl
Wooden spoon

## How To Make It

1. Combine cornbread crumbs in mixing bowl.
2. Melt butter or margarine in a frying pan.
3. Saute onions and celery.
4. Add egg and mix thoroughly with cornbread crumbs.
5. Add stock until the mixture is quite moist.
6. Add remaining ingredients; mix well.
7. Use stuffing to stuff turkey or bake in greased pan.
8. Bake at 400 degrees for 15 minutes.

Makes 6 cups

# FISH AND SEAFOOD
## *Fishing Time*

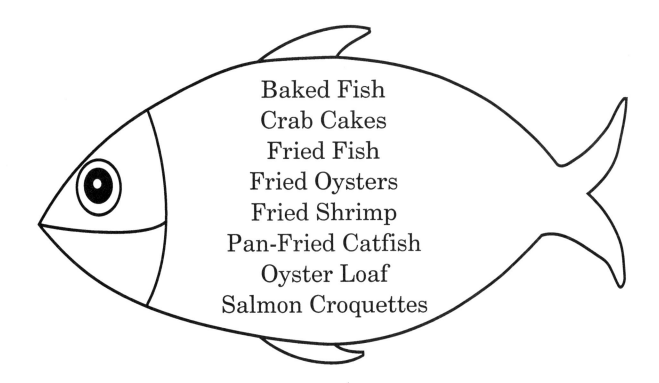

Baked Fish
Crab Cakes
Fried Fish
Fried Oysters
Fried Shrimp
Pan-Fried Catfish
Oyster Loaf
Salmon Croquettes

# BAKED FISH

## The INGREDIENTS I need

| | |
|---|---|
| 2 pounds | Fish Fillets (example: Catfish, Sole, Halibut, Trout) |
| 2 Tbsp. | Butter or Margarine, melted |
| 1/2 tsp. | Pepper |
| 1 tsp. | Salt |
| 1/2 tsp. | Paprika |
| 2 Tbsp. | Lemon Juice |
| 2 Tbsp. | Dried Parsley (optional) |

## The EQUIPMENT I need

Baking dish
Measuring spoons

## 8888888888888888 How To Make It 8888888888888888

1. Clean fish, wash cavity and dry.
2. Melt butter or margarine and spread evenly over the bottom of a baking dish.
3. Combine pepper, salt and paprika.
4. Sprinkle herb mixture on both sides of fish.
5. Place fish on top of butter.
6. Drizzle with lemon juice.
7. Garnish with parsley if desired.
8. Bake at 350 degrees for 15 to 20 minutes or until fish is almost done.

Serves 6

# CRAB CAKES

## The INGREDIENTS I need

2 cups     Crab Meat, cooked
2 Tbsp.    Butter or Margarine,
              melted
1 small    Onion, chopped fine
2            Eggs, beaten
1/2 cup    Bread Crumbs
1/2 tsp.    Salt
1/4 tsp.    Pepper
1 cup      Vegetable Oil for frying

## The EQUIPMENT I need

Skillet
Measuring cup/spoons
Bowl
Cutting board/knife

## ᪆᪆᪆᪆᪆᪆᪆᪆᪆᪆᪆᪆᪆᪆᪆ How To Make It ᪆᪆᪆᪆᪆᪆᪆᪆᪆᪆᪆᪆᪆᪆᪆

1. Saute chopped onions in butter.
2. In a bowl mix the crab, eggs, onions, bread crumbs, butter or margarine, salt and pepper together.
3. Shape into eight patties.
4. Fry in hot fat until golden brown 5 minutes.
5. Drain on a paper towel.

Serves 4

# FRIED FISH

## The INGREDIENTS I need

| | |
|---|---|
| 2 or 3 | Fish Pieces |
| 1 cup | Corn Meal, (white or yellow) |
| 1/8 tsp. | Salt |
| 1/8 tsp. | Pepper |
| 2 cups | Oil |

## The EQUIPMENT I need

Frying Pan
Measuring cup/spoons
Brown lunch bag or
plastic bag

## 8888888888888888 How To Make It 8888888888888888

1. Wash fish pieces.
2. Mix cornmeal, salt and pepper together.
3. Put fish in bag and shake until covered.
4. Drop fish in hot oil.
5. Fry until golden brown on both sides—3 minutes.
6. Serve with favorite sauce (ketchup or tartar).

Serves 3

# FRIED OYSTERS

## The INGREDIENTS I need

1 quart  Oysters
2  Eggs, beaten
1 cup  Cracker Meal or Bread
  Crumbs
1 Tbsp.  Water
Oil for frying

Salt and Pepper to taste

## The EQUIPMENT I need

Measuring cup/spoons
Bowl
Skillet

8888888888888888 **How To Make It** 888888888888888

1. Season oysters with salt and pepper.
2. Beat the eggs and add water.
3. Dip oysters into eggs.
4. Then dip into cracker meal or bread crumbs.
5. Fry in hot oil until golden—5 minutes.
6. Drain on paper towel.

Serves 5

# FRIED SHRIMP

## The INGREDIENTS I need

| | |
|---|---|
| 1 pound | Shrimp, shelled and deveined |
| 2 Tbsp. | Water, cold |
| 1 cup | Yellow Cornmeal |
| 1/2 tsp. | Salt |
| 1 | Egg |
| 1 cup | Vegetable Oil for frying |

## The EQUIPMENT I need

Skillet
Mixing bowl
Measuring cup/spoons

8888888888888888 **How To Make It** 8888888888888888

1. Beat egg with the water.
2. Combine cornmeal and salt.
3. Dip shrimp in the egg mixture.
4. Roll the shrimp in corn meal until coated.
5. Preheat skillet with oil.
6. Fry in deep oil to a golden brown.
7. Drain on paper towel.

Serves 4

# PAN-FRIED CATFISH

## The INGREDIENTS I need

1 pound Catfish Fillets
1 cup White Cornmeal
1/2 tsp. Salt
1/2 tsp. Pepper
1 cup Vegetable Oil for frying

## The EQUIPMENT I need

Brown lunch bag
Measuring cup/spoons
Skillet

## ᙖᙖᙖᙖᙖᙖᙖᙖᙖᙖᙖ How To Make It ᙖᙖᙖᙖᙖᙖᙖᙖᙖᙖᙖ

1. Put cornmeal, salt and pepper in a brown paper bag.
2. Add the fish to the bag and shake completely.
3. Heat oil in skillet—5 minutes.
4. Add fish and fry until golden brown on both sides—5 minutes.
5. Drain on paper towel.

Serves 3-4

# OYSTER LOAF

## The INGREDIENTS I need

| | |
|---|---|
| 10-12 | Oysters, raw |
| 1/2 tsp. | Salt |
| 1/2 tsp. | Paprika |
| 1/2 tsp. | Seasoning Salt |
| 2 | Eggs, beaten |
| 1 tsp. | Butter or Margarine |
| 1 tsp. | Worcestershire Sauce |
| 1 | Full loaf of Yeast Bread or French Bread |

## The EQUIPMENT I need

Measuring spoons
Bowl
Cookie sheet
Foil

## ꙮꙮꙮꙮꙮꙮꙮꙮꙮꙮꙮꙮ How To Make It ꙮꙮꙮꙮꙮꙮꙮꙮꙮꙮꙮꙮ

1. In a bowl mix oysters, salt, seasoning salt, paprika, eggs, butter and Worcestershire sauce together
2. Cut off end of bread loaf and scoop out inside.
3. Stuff ingredients into the loaf and wrap in foil.
4. Bake in oven for 20 minutes at 350 degrees.

**Serves 5**

# SALMON CROQUETTES

## The INGREDIENTS I need

| | |
|---|---|
| 1 15-1/2 oz. can | Pink Salmon |
| 2 | Eggs, beaten |
| 1/2 cup | Onions, chopped |
| 1 tsp. | Salt |
| 1/2 tsp. | Pepper |
| 3 Tbsp. | Flour |
| 1 cup | Vegetable Oil |

## The EQUIPMENT I need

Bowl
Egg beater
Measuring cup/spoons
Skillet
Cutting board/knife

ᵟᵟᵟᵟᵟᵟᵟᵟᵟᵟᵟᵟᵟᵟᵟᵟᵟ How To Make It ᵟᵟᵟᵟᵟᵟᵟᵟᵟᵟᵟᵟᵟᵟᵟᵟᵟ

1. Drain salmon.
2. Mix salmon, salt, pepper, eggs and flour in bowl.
3. Chop onions and add to bowl.
4. Mix all ingredients well.
5. Roll into patties.
6. Heat oil in skillet.
7. Place salmon patties in skillet.
8. Brown evenly on both sides.

Serves 5

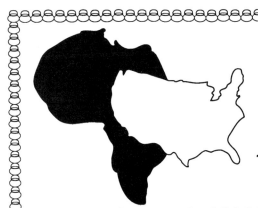

# PORK

## *Eatin' High on the Hog*

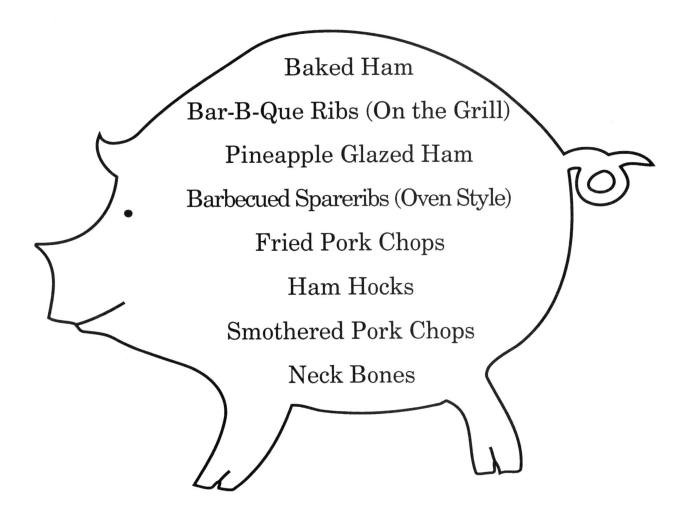

Baked Ham

Bar-B-Que Ribs (On the Grill)

Pineapple Glazed Ham

Barbecued Spareribs (Oven Style)

Fried Pork Chops

Ham Hocks

Smothered Pork Chops

Neck Bones

# BAKED HAM

## The INGREDIENTS I need

| | |
|---|---|
| 2-4 pounds | Ham |
| 6 whole | Cloves |
| 1/2 cup | Brown Sugar |
| 1 Tbsp. | Dry Mustard |

## The EQUIPMENT I need

Rack
Roasting Pan
Measuring cup/spoons

∞∞∞∞∞∞∞∞∞∞∞∞∞∞∞ **How To Make It** ∞∞∞∞∞∞∞∞∞∞∞∞∞∞∞

1. Preheat oven to 325 degrees.
2. Place ham with fat side up on rack in a shallow open roasting pan.
3. Stick cloves onto top and sides of the ham.
4. Mix brown sugar and mustard and spread mixture on surface of ham.
5. Bake 35 minutes per pound.
6. Serve hot or cold.

**Serves 4-6**

# BAR-B-QUE RIBS (On the Grill)

## The INGREDIENTS I need

2 pounds  Spareribs
1/2 tsp.  Salt
1 tsp.  Vinegar
2 quarts  Water
  Barbecue Sauce
  (See Sauce)

## The EQUIPMENT I need

Pot/lid
Measuring cup/spoons
Barbecue Grill
Charcoal
Charcoal lighter
Tongs/big fork
Brush for basting

## How To Make It

1. Place the ribs, salt, vinegar and water in the pot.
2. Bring to a boil and cover for 10 minutes.
3. Simmer for 30 minutes. Drain.
4. Place ribs on a hot barbecue grill and cook 15 minutes, turning at 10 minutes.
5. Baste with barbecue sauce until browned and done.

Serves 3-6

# PINEAPPLE GLAZED HAM

## The INGREDIENTS I need

| | |
|---|---|
| 5 to 6 pounds | Ham, fully cooked |
| 1/4 cup | Brown Sugar |
| 2 Tbsp. | Cornstarch |
| 1-1/2 cups | Pineapple Juice |
| 1 Tbsp. | Orange Peel, grated |
| 1/4 tsp. | Dry Mustard |
| Slices | Pineapple (optional) |
| | Cherries (optional) |

## The EQUIPMENT I need

Roasting pan
Pot
Measuring cup/spoons
Wooden spoon
Pastry Brush

ᙿᙿᙿᙿᙿᙿᙿᙿᙿᙿᙿᙿᙿ **How To Make It** ᙿᙿᙿᙿᙿᙿᙿᙿᙿᙿᙿᙿᙿ

1. Preheat oven to 325 degrees.
2. Bake ham in roasting pan for 2 hours.
3. Stir sugar with cornstarch in saucepan.
4. Add remaining ingredients.
5. Cook over medium heat, stirring occasionally until mixture thickens; remove from heat.
6. Last 30 minutes brush with orange mixture.
7. Garnish with pineapple slices and maraschino cherries.

Serves 10-12

# BARBECUED SPARERIBS (Oven Style)

## The INGREDIENTS I need

| | |
|---|---|
| 2 pounds | Spareribs |
| 2 cups | Sauce |
| | (See Sauces) |

## The EQUIPMENT I need

Baking pan
Measuring cup
Cutting board/knife

888888888888888 **How To Make It** 88888888888888

1. Place ribs in a shallow baking pan and roast at 450 degrees for 30 minutes.
2. Pour off the fat and reduce heat to 350 degrees.
3. Pour 1 cup of Barbecue Sauce over the ribs.
4. Bake, uncovered for 1-1/2 hours, until ribs are tender, basting occasionally.
5. Separate ribs with sharp knife.
6. Serve with sauce.

**Serves 3-6**

# FRIED PORK CHOPS

## The INGREDIENTS I need

| | |
|---|---|
| 4 | Pork Chops |
| 1/2 cup | Flour |
| 1/8 tsp. | Salt |
| 1/8 tsp. | Pepper |
| 2 cups | Oil (for frying) |

## The EQUIPMENT I need

Frying Pan
Measuring cup/spoons
Brown lunch bag or
plastic bag

ꝏꝏꝏꝏꝏꝏꝏꝏꝏꝏꝏꝏꝏ **How To Make It** ꝏꝏꝏꝏꝏꝏꝏꝏꝏꝏꝏꝏꝏ

1. Wash pork chops.
2. Mix flour, salt and pepper together.
3. Put chops in bag and shake until covered.
4. Drop chops in hot oil.
5. Fry until golden brown for 20 minutes.
6. Drain on paper towels.

**Serves 2-4**

# HAM HOCKS

## The INGREDIENTS I need

| | |
|---|---|
| 2-4 | Ham Hocks |
| | (Allow 1 per person) |
| Pinch | Salt |

## The EQUIPMENT I need

Pot/lid
Baking Dish

### ♒♒♒♒♒♒♒♒♒♒♒♒♒ How To Make It ♒♒♒♒♒♒♒♒♒♒♒♒♒

1. Put hock in a large pot.
2. Add just enough water to cover.
3. Add a pinch of salt.
4. Cover the pan and bring to a boil.
5. Reduce heat and simmer 2-1/2 to 3 hours until hocks are tender.
6. Put hocks in a baking dish.
7. Place in 450 degree oven to brown and dry out excess fat. Serve with greens.

Serves 2-4

# SMOTHERED PORK CHOPS

## The INGREDIENTS I need

| | |
|---|---|
| 3-4 | Pork Chops |
| 1 Tbsp. | Oil |
| 1 large | Onion, chopped |
| 1 clove | Garlic, minced |
| 1 tsp. | Flour |
| 1/2 tsp. | Parsley, chopped |
| 1/8 tsp. | Thyme |
| 1 | Bay Leaf |

Salt and Pepper to taste

## The EQUIPMENT I need

Skillet
Measuring spoons
Cutting board/knife

8888888888888888 **How To Make It** 8888888888888888

1. Season meat with salt and pepper.
2. Lightly dust with flour.
3. Fry meat in oil until golden brown on both sides.
4. Remove from pan and keep warm.
5. Add onions and garlic to the pan and brown.
6. Stir in one teaspoon of flour and brown.
7. Replace chops in the pan.
8. Add water to cover.
9. Add remaining ingredients.
10. Simmer uncovered, low flame for 30 to 40 minutes until chops are tender.

**Serves 2-4**

# NECK BONES

## The INGREDIENTS I need

| | |
|---|---|
| 3 pounds | Pork Neck bones |
| 1 cube | Beef or Chicken Bouillon |
| 1 Tbsp. | Salt |
| 4 cups | Water |
| 1 cup | Onions, chopped |
| 1/2 tsp. | Pepper |
| 3 | Carrots, fresh, peeled and halved |
| 1/2 tsp. | Thyme leaves |

## The EQUIPMENT I need

Pot/lid
Measuring cup/spoons
Cutting board/knife

## ଚଚଚଚଚଚଚଚଚଚଚଚଚଚ How To Make It ଚଚଚଚଚଚଚଚଚଚଚଚଚଚ

1. Wash neck bones in cold water.
2. Add 4 cups of water to pot.
3. Add neck bones, bouillon cube, onions, salt, pepper and thyme.
4. Cover pot and bring to rapid boil.
5. Simmer meat until tender and pulls away from bones easily— about 1-1/2 to 2 hours.
6. Add carrots the last 1/2 hour of cooking.

**Serves 4-6**

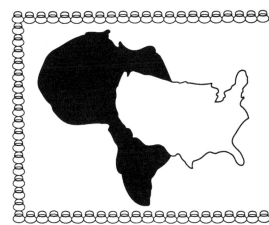

# SAUCES AND GRAVIES
## *Po'-it-on & Sop-it-up*

Brown Gravy

Cream Gravy

Giblet Gravy

Red Eye Gravy

Barbecue Sauce

# BROWN GRAVY

## The INGREDIENTS I need

| | |
|---|---|
| 2 Tbsp. | Fat |
| 3 Tbsp. | Flour |
| 1/4 tsp. | Salt |
| 1/8 tsp. | Pepper |
| 1-1/2 cup | Water, cold |

## The EQUIPMENT I need

Skillet
Wooden spoon
Measuring cup/spoons

## ଚଚଚଚଚଚଚଚଚଚଚଚଚଚଚ How To Make It ଚଚଚଚଚଚଚଚଚଚଚଚଚଚଚ

1. Heat fat in skillet.
2. Add flour, salt and pepper.
3. Stir until brown.
4. Add cold water.
5. Simmer for 5 minutes.

Makes 4-5 servings

# CREAM GRAVY

## The INGREDIENTS I need

2 Tbsp.    Butter
2 Tbsp.    Flour
1 cup      Milk
Pinch      Salt and Pepper

## The EQUIPMENT I need

Skillet
Wooden spoon
Measuring cup/spoons

ᴆᴆᴆᴆᴆᴆᴆᴆᴆᴆᴆᴆᴆᴆᴆ **How To Make It** ᴆᴆᴆᴆᴆᴆᴆᴆᴆᴆᴆᴆᴆᴆᴆ

1. Melt butter in skillet.
2. Stir in flour until well blended.
3. Add milk.
4. Season to taste.
5. Simmer for 5 minutes.

Makes 2-4 servings

# GIBLET GRAVY

## The INGREDIENTS I need

Gizzard, Neck, Liver of
      a chicken or turkey
3 cups    Water
1/2 tsp.   Salt
1/2        Onion, chopped
4 Tbsp.   Drippings from roasting pan (fat)
3 Tbsp.   Flour

## The EQUIPMENT I need

Skillet
Wooden spoon
Measuring cup/spoons
Cutting board/knife

## &#9758;&#9758;&#9758; How To Make It &#9758;&#9758;&#9758;

1. Place gizzard and neck in pot.
2. Add water, salt and onions.
3. Cover and boil for 1 hour.
4. In skillet add dripping from roasting pan.
5. Add flour in the fat, stir constantly.
6. Slowly stir in 1 cup of stock from the giblets.
7. Stir in 1 cup of water.
8. Chop up the giblets; add to gravy.
9. Simmer over low heat for 5 minutes.

**Makes 2 cups**

# RED EYE GRAVY

## The INGREDIENTS I need

1 Tbsp. Ham Fat
1 Tbsp. Flour
1/2 cup Water or
strong Coffee

## The EQUIPMENT I need

Skillet
Wooden spoon
Measuring cup/spoons

8888888888888888 **How To Make It** 8888888888888888

1. Stir the flour into the ham drippings in the skillet.
2. Add the water or coffee and stir until the gravy thickens, (10 minutes) (red looking).
3. Pour gravy over ham, grits or biscuits.

Makes 2-4 servings

# BARBECUE SAUCE

## The INGREDIENTS I need

| | |
|---|---|
| 2 Tbsp. | Butter or Margarine |
| 1 medium | Onion, chopped |
| 1 clove | Garlic, minced |
| 3/4 cup | Water |
| 1 cup | Tomato Catsup or Sauce |
| 2 Tbsp. | Vinegar |
| 2 Tbsp. | Lemon Juice |
| 2 Tbsp. | Worcestershire Sauce |
| 2 Tbsp. | Brown Sugar or Molasses |
| 1 tsp. | Dry Mustard |
| 1 tsp. | Salt |
| 1/4 tsp. | Pepper |
| 1/4 tsp. | Tabasco |
| Dash | Cayenne Pepper |

## The EQUIPMENT I need

Pot
Cutting board/knife
Measuring cup/spoons

## ∞∞∞∞∞∞∞∞∞∞∞∞∞∞∞ How To Make It ∞∞∞∞∞∞∞∞∞∞∞∞∞∞∞

1. Melt butter and add onion. Cook until brown.
2. Add rest of ingredients to pot.
3. Cook 20 minutes.

Makes 2 cups

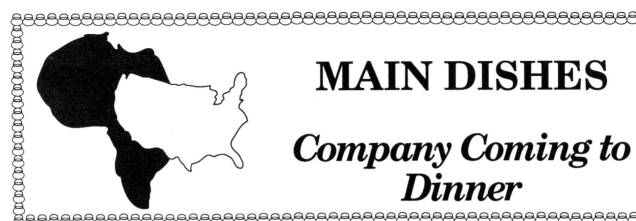

# MAIN DISHES

## Company Coming to Dinner

Baked Beans

Beef Stew

Brunswick Stew

Chili and Beans

Spaghetti
(with Meat Sauce)

Macaroni and Cheese

Turkey Hash

White Rice

# BAKED BEANS

## The INGREDIENTS I need

| | |
|---|---|
| 2 large cans | Pork and Beans |
| 1 small | Onion, chopped |
| 1-1/2 T. | Mustard |
| 2 T. | Molasses |
| 4 T. | Brown Sugar |
| 4 T. | Catsup or Barbecue Sauce |
| 2 T. | Corn Syrup |
| 1 /4 pound | Salt pork, diced or 6 slices bacon |
| 1tsp. | Salt |
| 1/2 tsp. | Pepper |

## The EQUIPMENT I need

Can opener
Measuring Spoon
Knife/Cutting board
Wooden spoon
Pan

ꂃꂃꂃꂃꂃꂃꂃꂃꂃꂃꂃꂃꂃꂃꂃ **How To Make It** ꂃꂃꂃꂃꂃꂃꂃꂃꂃꂃꂃꂃꂃꂃꂃ

1. Pour beans into pan.
2. Add onions, mustard, molasses, brown sugar, catsup, corn syrup, bacon, salt and pepper. Mix well.  Bake in oven for 1 hour at 350 degrees.

Serves 6-8

# BEEF STEW

## The INGREDIENTS I need

| | |
|---|---|
| 1 pound | Beef Stew Meat |
| 2 cups | Water |
| 1/2 tsp. | Salt |
| 1/2 tsp. | Pepper |
| 1/2 tsp. | Seasoned Salt |
| 2 | Potatoes, cubed |
| 2 | Carrots, cubed |
| 1 medium | Onion, chopped |
| 1 large can | Whole Tomatoes |
| 1 Tbsp. | Vegetable Oil |

## The EQUIPMENT I need

Pot/Lid
Measuring cup/spoons
Cutting board/knife
Wooden spoon

ꙮꙮꙮꙮꙮꙮꙮꙮꙮꙮꙮ **How To Make It** ꙮꙮꙮꙮꙮꙮꙮꙮꙮꙮꙮ

1. Brown the meat in hot oil.
2. Add water, salt, pepper, seasoned salt and onions.
3. Cover, Cook low for 1 hour, stirring occasionally.
4. Add carrots, potatoes and tomatoes.
5. Cover and cook for 30 minutes until vegetables are done.

**Serves 3**

# BRUNSWICK STEW

## The INGREDIENTS I need

| | |
|---|---|
| 2 Tbsp. | Bacon Fat |
| 2-1/2 pounds | Chicken or Rabbit |
| 2 medium | Onions, chopped |
| 6 cups | Chicken Broth or Water |
| 2 large | Potatoes, cubed |
| 1 clove | Garlic, minced |
| 1 | Bay Leaf |
| 1/2 tsp. | Dried Oregano |
| 1 10-oz. Pkg. | Frozen Lima Beans |
| 1 10-oz. Pkg. | Corn |
| 4 | Tomatoes, quartered |

Salt and Pepper to taste

## The EQUIPMENT I need

Pot
Measuring cup/spoons
Cutting board/knife
Wooden spoon

## How To Make It

1. Pat rabbit or chick pieces dry and season with salt and pepper.
2. Add chicken or rabbit to bacon fat and brown lightly on all sides for 10 minutes.
3. Add broth and bring to a boil. Simmer for 15 minutes.
4. Add remaining ingredients. Simmer for 30-40 minutes until meat and vegetables are tender.

Serves 4-6

# CHILI AND BEANS

## The INGREDIENTS I need

| | |
|---|---|
| 1 large can | Tomato Paste |
| 1 8-oz. can | Tomato Sauce |
| 1 pound | Ground Beef or |
| | Ground Turkey |
| 1 medium | Onion, chopped |
| 1 small | Green Pepper, chopped |
| 1 clove | Garlic, crushed |
| 1/8 tsp. | Salt and Pepper |
| 1 pound can | Kidney or Pinto Beans |
| 1 pkg. | Chili Seasoning or |
| 3 Tbsp. | Chili Powder |

## The EQUIPMENT I need

Pot
Measuring spoons
Wooden spoon
Cutting board/knife
Can opener

## ვვვვვვვვვვვვვვვ How To Make It ვვვვვვვვვვვვვვვ

1. Place paste, sauce, ground beef or turkey, onion peppers, garlic, salt and pepper into pot.
2. Cook covered over low heat stirring frequently until meat breaks into fine pieces.
3. Add chili seasoning mixing thoroughly.
4. Simmer for 30 minutes.
5. Add beans, stir and simmer another 20 minutes.
6. Serve with rice.

**Serves 4-6**

# MACARONI AND CHEESE

## The INGREDIENTS I need

1 8 oz. bag  Macaroni
8 cups      Boiling Water
1 tsp.      Salt
1 cup       Cheese, cubed
1/2 tsp.    Pepper
1 stick     Butter
2 cups      Milk
3           Eggs

## The EQUIPMENT I need

Pot
Measuring cup/spoons
Bowl
Wooden spoon
Casserole dish
Cutting board/knife

## ଶଶଶଶଶଶଶଶଶଶଶଶ How To Make It ଶଶଶଶଶଶଶଶଶଶଶଶ

1. Cook macaroni in boiling water until tender for 15 minutes.
2. Drain macaroni and place in casserole dish.
3. Add milk, eggs, butter, salt and pepper.
4. Add cheese.
5. Bake at 350 degrees for 40 minutes.

**Serves 6**

# SPAGHETTI (with Meat Sauce)

## The INGREDIENTS I need

| | |
|---|---|
| 1 | Onion, chopped |
| 2 Tbsp. | Olive Oil |
| 1 pound | Ground Beef or Ground Turkey |
| 1 tsp. | Salt |
| 1/4 tsp. | Pepper |
| 1 | Garlic Clove, crushed |
| 1 can | Tomato Paste (6 oz.) |
| 1 jar/can | Spaghetti Sauce, large |
| 1/2 tsp. | Basil |
| 1/2 tsp. | Oregano |
| 1 pound | Spaghetti |

## The EQUIPMENT I need

Large skillet
Large pot
Measuring spoons
Wooden spoon
Cutting board/knife
Colander
Can opener

## ᗺᗺᗺᗺᗺᗺᗺᗺᗺᗺᗺᗺᗺᗺᗺ How To Make It ᗺᗺᗺᗺᗺᗺᗺᗺᗺᗺᗺᗺᗺᗺᗺ

1. Brown onion in hot oil. Add meat and seasoning.
2. Brown lightly. Cover and simmer 10 minutes.
3. Add sauces, cover and simmer 45 minutes.
4. Cook spaghetti in boiling water with 1 teaspoon salt and 2 tablespoons of olive oil until tender 10-15 minutes.
5. Pour cold water over spaghetti in colander.
6. Drain. Serve spaghetti with sauce.
7. Sprinkle with parmesan cheese if you wish.

**Serves 4-6**

# TURKEY HASH

## The INGREDIENTS I need

2 Tbsp.   Butter or Margarine
1 cup     Onion, chopped
1/2 cup   Green Pepper, chopped
2 cups    Turkey, cooked, diced
2 cups    Potatoes, cooked and diced
1/2 tsp.  Salt
1/4 tsp.  Pepper
1 cup     Evaporated Milk
1/2 cup   Turkey Stock

## The EQUIPMENT I need

Large saucepan
Measuring cup/spoons
Cutting board/knife
Wooden spoon

## ∞∞∞∞∞∞∞∞∞∞∞∞∞∞ How To Make It ∞∞∞∞∞∞∞∞∞∞∞∞∞∞

1. Heat butter or margarine in large saucepan on medium heat.
2. Add onions and green peppers. Saute for 5 minutes.
3. Remove from heat. Stir in turkey, potatoes, salt and pepper.
4. Add evaporated milk and turkey stock gradually, stirring gently.
5. Cook until sauce is thick.
6. Serve over rice or toast.

Serves 4-6

# WHITE RICE

## The INGREDIENTS I need

## The EQUIPMENT I need

| | | |
|---|---|---|
| 1 Cup | Long Grain White Rice | Pot/lid |
| 1-1/2 cups | Cold Water | Measuring cup/spoons |
| 1 Tbsp. | Butter | |
| 1/2 tsp. | Salt | |

ᵹᵹᵹᵹᵹᵹᵹᵹᵹᵹᵹᵹᵹᵹᵹᵹ **How To Make It** ᵹᵹᵹᵹᵹᵹᵹᵹᵹᵹᵹᵹᵹᵹᵹᵹᵹ

1. Wash rice thoroughly.
2. Bring water, butter, rice and salt to boil in pot.
3. Cover with lid.
4. Simmer for 30 minutes.
5. Do not remove lid during cooking.

Serves 4

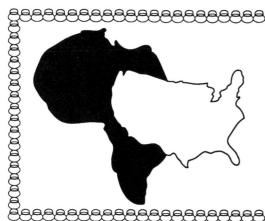

# CAKES, COOKIES AND PIES

## *Sweet Tradition*

Buttermilk Poundcake
Chocolate Cake & Icing
Coconut Cake & 7-Minute Icing
Holiday Fruitcake
Gingerbread Cake
Molasses Cake
Pineapple Upside-Down Cake
Pound Cake

Icebox Cookies
Shortnin' Bread
Sugar Cookies
Tea Cakes

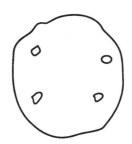

Apple Pies
Fried Pies
Lemon Pies
Lemon Meringue Pie
Pecan Pie
Sweet Potato Pie
Pie Crust

# BUTTERMILK POUNDCAKE

## The INGREDIENTS I need

| | |
|---|---|
| 3 cups | Flour |
| 1/2 tsp. | Soda |
| 1/2 tsp. | Baking Powder |
| 1/4 tsp. | Salt |
| 1/2 cup | Shortening |
| 1/2 cup | Butter |
| | or Margarine |
| 2 cups | Sugar |
| 4 | Eggs |
| 1 tsp | Vanilla Extract |
| 1 tsp. | Lemon Extract |
| 1 cup | Buttermilk |

## The EQUIPMENT I need

Tube pan
Measuring cups/spoons
Sifter
Bowl
Wooden spoon
Hand mixer
Timer

## 88888888888888888 How To Make It 88888888888888888

1. Sift together flour, soda, baking powder and salt.
2. Cream shortening and butter or margarine and sugar until light and fluffy.
3. Add eggs one at a time, beating well after each addition.
4. Add vanilla and lemon extracts; mix well.
5. Add flour mixture alternately with the buttermilk. Beat well.
6. Bake in a tube pan at 325 degrees for 1 hour 15 minutes.

Serves 8-10

# CHOCOLATE CAKE

## The INGREDIENTS I need

| | |
|---|---|
| 3 squares | Unsweetened Chocolate |
| 1/2 cup | Water |
| 2 cups | Flour, sifted |
| 1-1/2 tsp. | Baking Powder |
| 1 tsp. | Baking Soda |
| 1 tsp. | Salt |
| 2/3 cup | Butter or Margarine |
| 1-2/3 cups | Sugar |
| 3 | Eggs |
| 1 tsp. | Vanilla |
| 1 cup | Buttermilk |

## The EQUIPMENT I need

Saucepan
Measuring cups/spoons
Sifter
Bowl/wooden spoon
Hand mixer
9-inch cake pans
Rubber spatula
Timer

## ∞∞∞∞∞∞∞∞∞∞∞∞∞ How To Make It ∞∞∞∞∞∞∞∞∞∞∞∞∞

1. Preheat over to 350 degrees
2. Melt chocolate in water. Cool.
3. Sift flour, baking powder, soda and salt together.
4. Cream butter or margarine and sugar
5. Add eggs and vanilla; mix well.
6. Blend in the buttermilk and cooled chocolate.
7. Stir in the flour mixture.
8. Pour batter into 2 well-greased 9-inch layer pans.
9. Bake for 35 minutes.
10. Cool and frost with Chocolate Icing.*

Serves 8-10

*See Chocolate Icing recipe on next page.

# CHOCOLATE ICING

## The INGREDIENTS I need

1/2 cup   Butter
1/2 cup   Cocoa
2 cups   Sugar
1/2 cup   Milk
1/3 cup   Light Corn Syrup
1 tsp.   Vanilla

## The EQUIPMENT I need

Saucepan
Measuring cup/spoons
Wooden spoon

## ᕼᕼᕼᕼᕼᕼᕼᕼᕼᕼᕼᕼᕼᕼᕼ How To Make It ᕼᕼᕼᕼᕼᕼᕼᕼᕼᕼᕼᕼᕼᕼ

1. Melt butter in saucepan.
2. Add remaining ingredients
3. Bring to boil and cook one minute
4. Cool. Beat to desired consistency.
5. Frosts 2-layer 9-inch cake.

# COCONUT CAKE

## The INGREDIENTS I need

| | |
|---|---|
| 3 cups | Sugar |
| 2 sticks | Butter or Margarine |
| 3 cups | Flour |
| 1/2 tsp. | Salt |
| 1-1/2 tsp. | Vanilla |
| 5 | Eggs |
| 1/2 tsp. | Baking Powder |
| 1 cup | Milk |
| 1/2 tsp. | Almond Flavoring |

## The EQUIPMENT I need

Bowl
Measuring cups/spoons
Wooden spoon
3 cake pans
Electric mixer

## ᔆᔆᔆᔆᔆᔆᔆᔆᔆᔆᔆᔆᔆᔆᔆ How To Make It ᔆᔆᔆᔆᔆᔆᔆᔆᔆᔆᔆᔆᔆᔆᔆ

1. Cream softened butter or margarine, sugar and egg together in a bowl.
2. Combine dry ingredients and add alternately with milk.
3. Add flavoring and mix well.
4. Bake in 3 greased and floured cake pans at 325 degrees for 40 minutes.
5. The 7-minute icing recipe on the next page makes enough for 3-layer cake.

# SEVEN-MINUTE ICING

## The INGREDIENTS I need

| | |
|---|---|
| 1-1/2 Cup | Sugar |
| 2 | Egg Whites |
| 1/2 tsp. | Cream of Tartar |
| 1/2 cup | Boiling Water |
| 1 pkg. | Flaked Coconut |

## The EQUIPMENT I need

Double boiler
Measuring cup/spoons
Electric mixer
Rubber spatula

## ⛯⛯⛯⛯⛯⛯⛯⛯⛯⛯⛯ How To Make It ⛯⛯⛯⛯⛯⛯⛯⛯⛯⛯⛯

1. Combine all ingredients except the water in the top of a double boiler.
2. Blend with an electric mixer on low speed.
3. Add the boiling water gradually, stirring constantly and continue cooking in double boiler.
4. Beat at high speed of electric mixer until icing is firm and stands in peaks.
5. Spread on cake with 2 cups flaked coconut.

# HOLIDAY FRUITCAKE

## The INGREDIENTS I need

| | |
|---|---|
| 1-1/2 pound | Raisins |
| 1/4 pound | Currants |
| 1/2 c. Dark | Rum or Brandy |
| 1/4 pound | Butter (room temp.) |
| 1 cup | White Sugar |
| 1 cup | Dark Brown Sugar |
| 5 | Eggs (Room Temp.) |
| 2 cups | Cake Flour, sifted |
| 2 tsp. | Baking Powder |
| 1 T. | Orange Juice |
| 1tsp. | Almond Extract |
| 1pound | Candied Fruits, chopped |
| 1 cup | Chopped Walnuts or Pecans |

## The EQUIPMENT I need

Bowl
Measuring cup/spoons
Sifter
Wooden spoon
9-inch pan or 2 loaf pans
Foil
Electric mixer

NOTE!    This recipe has alcohol in it. Make sure you have permission to make it before you start. It is also a good idea to have your grown-up helper handle the alcohol.

## ✇✇✇✇✇✇✇✇✇✇✇✇✇✇ How To Make It ✇✇✇✇✇✇✇✇✇✇✇✇✇✇

1.  Soak raisins and currants in the rum or other liquor for 1 hour or more.
2.  Preheat oven to 350°.
3.  Cream butter and sugar. Beat in eggs one at a time.
4.  Sift flour and baking powder together.
5.  Add rum-soaked raisins and currants to the egg-butter batter. Mix well.
6.  Alternately stir in flour and juice.
7.  Gently blend in extract, candied fruits and nuts.
8.  Pour batter into greased 9-inch or 2 loaf pans.
9.  Bake 45-60 minutes; remove from oven.
10.  Sprinkle with rum; let cool. Wrap in aluminum foil and age cake two weeks or longer.
11.  The cake will be moist and will develop a great flavor. Add additional rum or brandy.

Serves  8-10

# GINGERBREAD CAKE

## The INGREDIENTS I need

| | |
|---|---|
| 1 cup | Molasses |
| 1 cup | Brown Sugar |
| 1/2 cup | Melted Butter or Margarine |
| 2 | Eggs |
| 1 tsp. | Cinnamon |
| 1 tsp. | Ginger |
| 1 tsp. | Cloves |
| 1 tsp. | Baking Soda |
| 1 cup | Boiling water |
| 3 cups | Flour |

## The EQUIPMENT I need

Measuring cup/spoons
Bowl
Pot
Wooden Spoon
8" Square Pan

## ꙮꙮꙮꙮꙮꙮꙮꙮꙮꙮꙮ How To Make It ꙮꙮꙮꙮꙮꙮꙮꙮꙮꙮꙮ

1. Stir brown sugar into melted butter or margarine.
2. Add eggs, beat well.
3. Dissolve baking soda in boiling water.
4. Add spices.
5. Beat well and gradually add the flour.
6. Pour into 8-inch square pan.
7. Bake at 350 degrees for 25 minutes.

Serves 5-7

# MOLASSES CAKE

## The INGREDIENTS I need

| | |
|---|---|
| 1 cup | Butter or Margarine |
| 3/4 cup | Sugar |
| 3 | Eggs, beaten |
| 1 cup | Molasses |
| 3 cups | Flour |
| 1 tsp. | Baking Soda |
| 1 tsp. | Cinnamon |
| 1/2 tsp. | Nutmeg |
| 1/2 tsp. | Ground Cloves |
| 1/4 tsp. | Allspice or Ginger |
| 1 cup | Milk |
| 1/2 cup | Raisins |

## The EQUIPMENT I need

Measuring cup/spoons
Bowl
Wooden spoon
Sifter
Electric mixer
Loaf pan

### ꙮꙮꙮꙮꙮꙮꙮꙮꙮꙮꙮꙮꙮ How To Make It ꙮꙮꙮꙮꙮꙮꙮꙮꙮꙮꙮꙮꙮ

1. Preheat oven to 350 degrees.
2. Cream butter or margarine and sugar.
3. Beat in eggs and molasses.
4. Sift all dry ingredients together.
5. Alternately beat dry ingredients and milk, a little at a time, into the batter.
6. Mix well. Add raisins.
7. Pour into a greased loaf pan.
8. Bake 1 hour.

**Serves 4-6**

# PINEAPPLE UPSIDE-DOWN CAKE

## The INGREDIENTS I need

| | |
|---|---|
| 1/2 cup | Brown Sugar |
| 2 Tbsp. | Butter or Margarine |
| 1 can (30oz.) | Pineapple slices |
| 10 | Maraschino Cherries |
| 2 cups | Cake Flour, sifted |
| 2 Tbsp. | Baking Powder |
| 1/4 tsp. | Salt |
| 1/4 cup | Shortening |
| 1 cup | Sugar |
| 1 | Egg, beaten |
| 1 tsp. | Vanilla |
| 3/4 cup | Milk |

## The EQUIPMENT I need

11 x 14 inch pan
Measuring cup/spoons
Sifter
Bowl
Wooden spoon
Electric Beater

## ଈଈଈଈଈଈଈଈଈଈଈଈଈଈ How To Make It ଈଈଈଈଈଈଈଈଈଈଈଈଈଈ

1. Sprinkle brown sugar in bottom of well-greased pan. Dot with butter.
2. Drain pineapple.
3. Place slices in pan with cherry in center or each.
4. Sift together flour, baking powder and salt.
5. Cream shortening; add sugar gradually and beat until fluffy.
6. Add egg and vanilla and beat well.
7. Add flour mixture, a little at a time, alternately with milk.
8. Pour batter over fruit.
9. Bake at 350 degrees until brown. Turn upside down on serving plate.

Makes 8-10 servings

# POUND CAKE

## The INGREDIENTS I need

| | |
|---|---|
| 1 cup | Butter or Margarine |
| 2 cups | Sugar |
| 3 cups | Cake Flour, sifted |
| 1 tsp. | Baking Powder |
| 1/4 tsp. | Salt |
| 6 | Eggs, separated |
| 1 cup | Milk |
| 1 tsp. | Vanilla Flavoring |
| 1 tsp. | Lemon Flavoring |

## The EQUIPMENT I need

Hand mixer
Cake pan tube
Bowl
Wooden spoon
Measuring cup/spoons
Timer

## ᪵᪵᪵᪵᪵᪵᪵᪵᪵᪵᪵᪵᪵᪵ How To Make It ᪵᪵᪵᪵᪵᪵᪵᪵᪵᪵᪵᪵᪵᪵

1. Cream the butter or margarine and sugar.
2. Add the egg yolks; beat well.
3. Add sifted cake flour, salt and baking powder alternately with milk.
4. Add vanilla and lemon flavoring and stiffly beaten egg whites.
5. Bake in a greased tube pan at 350 degrees for 1 hour or until toothpick or cake tester comes out clean.

Makes 8-10 servings

# ICEBOX COOKIES

## The INGREDIENTS I need

| | |
|---|---|
| 2 cups | Flour |
| 1-1/2 tsp. | Baking Powder |
| 1/2 tsp. | Salt |
| 1/2 cup | Shortening |
| 1 cup | Sugar |
| 2 | Eggs |
| 1 cup | Coconut (shredded) |
| 1 Tbsp. | Milk |
| 1 tsp. | Vanilla |
| | Vegetable oil spray |

## The EQUIPMENT I need

Measuring cup/spoons
Sifter
Bowl
Wooden spoon
Waxed paper
Cookie sheet
Spatula

## &&&&&&&&&&&&&&&& How To Make It &&&&&&&&&&&&&&&&

1. Sift flour, baking powder and salt.
2. Cream shortening and sugar.
3. Add eggs, coconut, milk and vanilla.
4. Mix together and gradually add flour mixture.
5. Divide dough into two parts and shape into 2 rolls 1-1/2 inches.
6. Roll in waxed paper.
7. Chill until firm about 1 hour.
8. Cut into 1/4 inch slices.
9. Bake on lightly greased cookie sheet at 425 degrees for 5 minutes.

**Makes 7 dozen**

# SHORTNIN' BREAD

## The INGREDIENTS I need

| | |
|---|---|
| 2 cups | Flour, sifted |
| 1/2 cup | Light Brown Sugar |
| 1 cup | Butter or Margarine (at room temperature) |
| Few grains | Salt |
| | Vegetable Oil Spray |

## The EQUIPMENT I need

Measuring cup/spoons
Bowl
Wooden spoon
Sifter
Wax paper
Cutting board/knife
Cookie sheet

8888888888888888 **How To Make It** 8888888888888888

1. Preheat oven to 350 degrees.
2. Cream the butter or margarine.
3. Add and blend in the sugar.
4. Add flour and salt and work thoroughly with hands until smooth.
5. Place the dough on wax paper and pat to 1/2 inch thickness.
6. Chill for 30 minutes.
7. Cut into squares.
8. Bake on lightly greased cookie sheet for 25-30 minutes.

Makes 2 dozen

# SUGAR COOKIES

## The INGREDIENTS I need

| | |
|---|---|
| 1-1/2 cups | Flour, sifted |
| 1/2 tsp. | Baking Powder |
| 1/2 tsp. | Salt |
| 1/2 tsp. | Baking Soda |
| 2/3 cup | Sugar |
| 1/2 cup | Butter or Margarine |
| 2 | Eggs |
| 2 Tbsp. | Milk |
| 1 tsp. | Vanilla |

## The EQUIPMENT I need

Measuring cup/spoons
Bowl
Wooden spoon
Sifter
Cookie Sheet
Spatula

## ₴₴₴₴₴₴₴₴₴₴₴₴₴₴₴ How To Make It ₴₴₴₴₴₴₴₴₴₴₴₴₴₴₴

1. Preheat over to 350 degrees.
2. Sift the dry ingredient together.
3. Cream sugar, butter or margarine and eggs.
4. Add vanilla and milk; mix well.
5. Chill dough for 1 hour.
6. Drop dough by teaspoonfuls onto lightly greased cookie sheet.
7. Flatten the tops of the cookie with the spatula.
8. Bake 15 minutes.

**Makes 2 dozen**

# TEA CAKES

## The INGREDIENTS I need

| | |
|---|---|
| 2 cups | Sugar |
| 3 | Eggs |
| 1 cup | Milk |
| 1-1/2 tsp. | Baking Powder |
| 1-1/2 tsp. | Nutmeg |
| 3 cups | White Flour, sifted |
| 2 tsp. | Vanilla |

## The EQUIPMENT I need

Measuring cup/spoons
Electric mixer
Bowl
Wooden Spoon
Rolling Pin
Cutting Board
Biscuit Cutter
Baking Sheet

## 88888888888888888 How To Make It 88888888888888888

1. Beat sugar and eggs together for 10 minutes.
2. Add milk, baking powder, butter, nutmeg and vanilla
3. Roll onto a floured board and knead for about 5 minutes.
4. Cut into 1/2 inch biscuit rounds, roll out thin.
5. Bake at 350 degrees for 15 minutes.

Makes 30 cakes

# APPLE PIE

## The INGREDIENTS I need

| | |
|---|---|
| 6-8 | Apples |
| 1 cup | Sugar |
| | Juice and grated rind, |
| 1/2 | Lemon or |
| | 1 tsp. Lemon Juice |
| 4 Tbsp. | Butter or Margarine |
| 1/2 tsp. | Cinnamon |
| 1/4 tsp. | Nutmeg |
| 2 Tbsp. | Flour |
| Pinch | Salt |
| | Pastry for 9" double crust |

*See Pie Crust recipe on page 175.

## The EQUIPMENT I need

Apple Peeler
Grater
Measuring cup/spoons
9" pie pan
Cutting board/knife

## ᛪᛪᛪᛪᛪᛪᛪᛪᛪᛪᛪᛪᛪᛪ How To Make It ᛪᛪᛪᛪᛪᛪᛪᛪᛪᛪᛪᛪᛪᛪ

1. Wash and peel, core and slice thin apples.
2. Combine flour, sugar, spices and salt.
3. Mix with the apples.
4. Fill pastry shell with apples and dot with butter or margarine.
5. Cover with crust. Prick top with fork. Crimp edges of pie crust.
6. Bake at 400 degrees for 10 minutes.
7. Reduce heat to 350 degrees for 40 minutes until golden brown.

Serves 6-8

# FRIED PIES

## The INGREDIENTS I need

| | |
|---|---|
| 2 cups | Flour |
| 1/2 tsp. | Salt |
| 1 tsp. | Soda |
| 1/2 cup | Shortening |
| 1/2 cup | Ice Water |
| 2 cups | Canned sliced peaches drained or dried appples or Apricots |
| 1/4 tsp. | Nutmeg |
| 1/2 tsp. | Cinnamon |

## The EQUIPMENT I need

Fry pan
Sifter
Measuring cup/spoons
Rolling pin
Fork/spoon
Can opener
Paper towel
Waxed paper

## ᘓᘓᘓᘓᘓᘓᘓᘓᘓᘓᘓᘓᘓᘓᘓ How To Make It ᘓᘓᘓᘓᘓᘓᘓᘓᘓᘓᘓᘓᘓᘓᘓ

1. Sift dry ingredients together and cut in the shortening.
2. Sprinkle ice water over, working the dough lightly until the dough holds together.
3. Shape into a ball, wrap in waxed paper and chill.
4. Roll dough out and cut into large rounds.
5. Place fruit in center or each round.
6. Sprinkle with nutmeg and cinnamon.
7. Fold over and press edges together with a wet fork.
8. Fry in deep hot fat until golden brown for 3 minutes.
9. Drain on paper towels.

**Makes 12**

# LEMON PIE

## The INGREDIENTS I need

| | |
|---|---|
| 3 | Eggs, well beaten |
| 1/2 cup | Butter or Margarine, melted |
| 3 Tbsp. | Lemon Juice |
| 1 Tbsp. | Grated Lemon Rind |
| 1 cup | Sugar |
| 9" | Unbaked Pie Shell (Frozen from store) |

## The EQUIPMENT I need

Saucepan
Bowl
Wooden spoon
Measuring cup/spoons
Grater

## ᘓᘓᘓᘓᘓᘓᘓᘓᘓᘓᘓᘓᘓᘓᘓᘓ How To Make It ᘓᘓᘓᘓᘓᘓᘓᘓᘓᘓᘓᘓᘓᘓᘓᘓ

1. Preheat over to 325 degrees.
2. Blend all of the filling ingredients.
3. Pour into the pie shell.
4. Bake for 25 minutes.
5. Remove pie from oven. Let cool. The filling will congeal as it cools.

**Serves 4-6**

# LEMON MERINGUE PIE

## The INGREDIENTS I need

| | |
|---|---|
| 3 Tbsp. | Cornstarch |
| 3 Tbsp. | Flour |
| 1-1/2 cup | Boiling Water |
| 3 | Egg Yolks |
| 1 tsp. | Butter |
| Rind | Of 1 Lemon |
| 1/4 cup | Lemon Juice |
| 1/4 cup | Sugar |
| 9" | Pie Crust, baked |

## The EQUIPMENT I need

Double boiler
Measuring cup/spoons
Wooden spoon

## ᠘᠘᠘᠘᠘᠘᠘᠘᠘᠘᠘᠘᠘᠘᠘᠘ How To Make It ᠘᠘᠘᠘᠘᠘᠘᠘᠘᠘᠘᠘᠘᠘᠘᠘

1. Mix cornstarch, sugar, salt and flour.
2. Add slowly to boiling water beating well until smooth and thick.
3. Cook in double boiler 10 minutes.
4. Beat three egg yolks until light.
5. Add hot starch mixture to egg yolks a little at a time, beating until smooth.
6. Return to double boiler, add butter and cook 5 minutes.
7. Remove from heat.
8. Add lemon juice and rind.
9. Cool slightly and pour into baked pie crust.

**Makes 6-8 servings**

# MERINGUE

## The INGREDIENTS I need

3          Egg Whites
6 Tbsp.   Sugar

## The EQUIPMENT I need

Electric mixer
Measuring spoon

8888888888888888 **How To Make It** 8888888888888888

1. Beat egg whites until stiff but not dry.
2. Beat in 2/3 of sugar a little at a time.
3. Fold in remaining sugar.
4. Spread on top of pie filling.
5. Place in oven at 300 degrees for 10 minutes.

# PECAN PIE

## The INGREDIENTS I need

| | |
|---|---|
| 1/2 cup | Sugar |
| 1 stick | Butter |
| 1 cup | Light Corn Syrup |
| 3 | Eggs |
| Pinch | Of Salt |
| 1 cup | Chopped Pecans |
| 1 9" | Pie Shell, unbaked |

## The EQUIPMENT I need

Bowl
Measuring cups
Spoon

## ᪉᪉᪉᪉᪉᪉᪉᪉᪉᪉᪉᪉᪉᪉᪉ How To Make It ᪉᪉᪉᪉᪉᪉᪉᪉᪉᪉᪉᪉᪉᪉᪉

1. Preheat oven to 350 degrees.
2. Cream butter and sugar.
3. Add syrup and salt.
4. Beat in eggs, one at a time.
5. Add pecans.
6. Pour the mixture into pie shell.
7. Bake at 350 degrees for 50 minutes.

**Serves 4-6**

# SWEET POTATO PIE

## The INGREDIENTS I need

| | |
|---|---|
| 2 cups | Mashed Sweet Potato or Yams |
| 1/2 cup | Butter, melted |
| 3 | Eggs |
| 1 cup | Sugar |
| 1/2 cup | Brown Sugar |
| 1 tsp. | Nutmeg |
| 1 tsp. | Cinnamon |
| 1 tsp. | Vanilla |
| 1 cup | Evaporated Milk |
| 2 9" | Pie Crusts |

## The EQUIPMENT I need

Bowl
Measuring cup/spoons
Wooden Spoon
Spatula
Electric Beater

## How To Make It

1. Combine sweet potatoes and melted butter.
2. Add sugars and eggs.
3. Beat until smooth. Add milk, nutmeg, cinnamon and vanilla extract.
4. Beat well. Pour into pie shell.
5. Bake at 375 degrees for one hour.

Serves 6

# PIE CRUST

## The INGREDIENTS I need

| | |
|---|---|
| 1-1/2 cups | Sifted Flour |
| 1/2 tsp. | Salt |
| 1/2 cup | Shortening |
| 4 Tbsp. | Ice Water |
| Two 9-inch | Pie plates |

## The EQUIPMENT I need

Wooden spoon
Sifter
Measuring cup/spoons
Fork or pastry blender
Rolling pin
Bowl

## ৪৪৪৪৪৪৪৪৪৪৪৪৪৪৪ How To Make It ৪৪৪৪৪৪৪৪৪৪৪৪৪৪৪

1. Sift dry ingredient together.
2. Cut in shortening with pastry blender until pieces are the size of peas.
3. Add water gradually, mixing with fork until dough is moistened.
4. Roll out on floured board and cut into crusts to fit 9" pie plate.

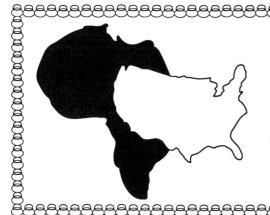

# DESSERTS
## *Old Fashioned Treats*

Apple Brown Betty
Peach Cobbler

### Puddings
Banana
Bread
Corn
Rice

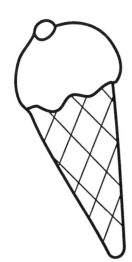

### Candy
Chocolate Fudge
Divinity
Penuche
Pralines

**Ice Cream -** Homemade Vanilla Ice Cream

# APPLE BROWN BETTY

## The INGREDIENTS I need

| | |
|---|---|
| 2 cups | Bread Crumbs |
| 1/4 cup | Melted Butter |
| 2 large | Apples |
| 3/4 cup | Sugar |
| 1/4 tsp. | Nutmeg |
| 1 tsp. | Lemon Juice |
| 1/2 cup | Hot Water |
| 1/2 tsp. | Almond Extract |

## The EQUIPMENT I need

Apple Corer
Knife
Measuring cup/spoons
Pot
Bowl
Baking pan

## ееееееееееееее How To Make It ееееееееееееее

1. Preheat oven to 350 degrees.
2. Peel apples, remove core and slice.
3. Mix together all the ingredients.
4. Pour batter into a buttered baking pan.
5. Cover and bake in oven for 25 minutes.
6. Remove cover, continue baking for 15 minutes.

**Serves 4-6**

# PEACH COBBLER

## The INGREDIENTS I need

| | |
|---|---|
| 2-1/2 cups | Sliced peaches, canned or fresh |
| 1 cup | Sugar |
| 1 tsp. | Nutmeg |
| 2 tsps. | Cinnamon |
| 1 Tbsp. or | Corn Starch |
| 2 Tbsp. | Flour |
| 1 stick | Butter or Margarine |
| 1 | Egg, beaten |

*See pie crust recipe on page 175

## The EQUIPMENT I need

9-inch pie pan
Measuring cup/spoon
Bowl
Wooden spoon
Cutting board/knife
Rolling pin
Fork

## ℮℮℮℮℮℮℮℮℮℮℮℮℮℮ How To Make It ℮℮℮℮℮℮℮℮℮℮℮℮℮℮

1. Preheat oven to 350 degrees.
2. Mix sugar, corn starch and spices together.
3. Add melted butter and mix well.
4. Roll pie dough, cover bottom and sides of pan with dough.
5. Pour in filling, cover top with remaining dough.
6. Poke fork holes into top dough before topping with beaten egg.
7. Bake for 45 minutes.  Serve hot or cold.

**Serves 4-6**

# CHOCOLATE FUDGE

## The INGREDIENTS I need

| | |
|---|---|
| 2 cups | Sugar |
| 1/2 cup | Butter |
| 1 can | Evaporated Milk |
| 2 squares | Unsweetened Chocolate |
| 1 tsp. | Vanilla |
| 1/2 cup | Nuts, chopped (Walnuts or Pecans) |

## The EQUIPMENT I need

Saucepan
Measuring cup/spoons
Shallow pan

## 88888888888888888 How To Make It 88888888888888888

1. Cook everything together, except nuts, over medium heat.
2. Stir to keep from burning.
3. When the mixture forms a soft ball in cold water, remove from heat.
4. Let cool. Beat and add nuts.
5. Spread in a buttered pan and cut.

Serves 6

# DIVINITY

## The INGREDIENTS I need

2-3/4 cups    Sugar
2/3 cup    White Karo Syrup
1/2 cup    Water
2    Egg Whites

## The EQUIPMENT I need

Saucepan
Measuring cup
Electric Mixer

## How To Make It

1. Boil to a soft ball stage first three ingredients.
   (Syrup is tested by dropping a drop of syrup in cold water until it forms a soft ball.)
2. Add half to egg whites, beaten stiff.
3. Cook other half to hard ball stage.
4. Then add to rest of mixture and beat until stiff.

Makes 24 pieces

# PENUCHE

## The INGREDIENTS I need

| | |
|---|---|
| 1-1/4 cups | Light Brown Sugar |
| 1 Tbsp. | Dark Syrup |
| 3/4 cup | Evaporated Milk |
| 1 Tbsp. | Butter or Margarine |
| Dash | Salt |
| 1/2 tsp. | Vanilla |
| 1 cup | Nuts, chopped (Pecan or Walnuts) |

## The EQUIPMENT I need

Saucepan
Wooden spoon
Square pan
Measuring cup/spoon

### ꙮꙮꙮꙮꙮꙮꙮꙮꙮꙮ How To Make It ꙮꙮꙮꙮꙮꙮꙮꙮꙮꙮ

1. In a saucepan mix sugar, corn syrup, milk and salt.
2. Stir over low heat until sugar dissolves and mixture boils.
3. Cook until candy makes a soft ball when dropped in cold water.
4. Add butter or margarine, cool mixture to lukewarm.
5. Stir in vanilla and beat until it becomes creamy.
6. Stir in nuts and pour the candy into a buttered pan.
7. Cut into squares when cold.

**Makes 18 pieces**

# PRALINES

## The INGREDIENTS I need

| | |
|---|---|
| 1 cup | White Sugar |
| 1 cup | Brown Sugar |
| 1 cup | Evaporated Milk |
| 1/4 tsp. | Salt |
| 1 Tbsp. | Butter or Margarine |
| 1 tsp. | Vanilla |
| 1/2 tsp. | Baking Soda |
| 2 cups | Pecan Halves |

## The EQUIPMENT I need

Heavy pot
Measuring cup/spoons
Candy thermometer
Waxed paper

## ᙚᙚᙚᙚᙚᙚᙚᙚᙚᙚᙚᙚᙚᙚ How To Make It ᙚᙚᙚᙚᙚᙚᙚᙚᙚᙚᙚᙚᙚᙚ

1. Mix sugars, evaporated milk, soda, salt and butter or margarine in heavy saucepan.
2. Cook over high heat (boil) for 5 minutes.
3. Stir until candy reaches soft ball stage about 5 minutes. (When candy thermometer reaches 236 degrees or when mixture forms a soft ball when dropped in cold water.)
4. Remove from heat and let cool slightly.
5. Add pecans and vanilla.
6. Beat until light and creamy.
7. Drop the candy on waxed paper in 3-inch patties and let cool.

**Makes 15-18**

# HOMEMADE VANILLA ICE CREAM

## The INGREDIENTS I need

| | |
|---|---|
| 2 cups | Sugar |
| 6 | Eggs |
| 1 quart | Milk |
| 1 cup | Cream |
| 2-12 oz. cans | Evaporated Milk |
| 3 tsp. | Vanilla |
| 1 tsp. | Salt |

## The EQUIPMENT I need

Saucepan
Wooden spoon
Measuring cup/spoons
Hand-crank or Electric
Ice Cream Maker

## How To Make It

1. Scald milk. Beat eggs; add sugar and salt.
2. Beat well until sugar is dissolved.
3. Cook mixture stirring continually over low fire.
4. Remove from heat and cool.
5. Add cream, evaporated milk and vanilla.
6. Pour into Ice Cream Maker and freeze until hard according to directions on Maker.

* For fresh fruit ice cream, add a pint of peaches, strawberries or other fresh fruit.

Makes 1 gallon

# BANANA PUDDING

## The INGREDIENTS I need

| | |
|---|---|
| 2/3 cup | Sugar |
| 1/3 cup | Cornstarch |
| 1/2 tsp. | Salt |
| 3 cups | Milk |
| 2 | Eggs |
| 3 Tbsp. | Butter or Margarine |
| 2 tsp. | Vanilla |
| 2 Cups | Vanilla Wafers |
| 2 cups | Ripe Bananas, sliced |

## The EQUIPMENT I need

Saucepan
Measuring cup/spoons
Wooden spoon
Casserole dish
Cutting board/knife

## ᲒᲒᲒᲒᲒᲒᲒᲒᲒᲒᲒᲒᲒᲒᲒᲒᲒᲒ How To Make It ᲒᲒᲒᲒᲒᲒᲒᲒᲒᲒᲒᲒᲒᲒᲒᲒ

1.  Combine sugar, cornstarch, salt and milk in a large saucepan.
2.  Cook over medium heat until thickened.
3.  Beat eggs lightly and add a little of the hot mixture to them.
4.  Blend well and pour into saucepan.
5.  Continue cooking, stirring constantly, for a few minutes.
6.  Add butter and vanilla and blend well.
7.  Cover pudding and cool slightly.
8.  Arrange vanilla wafers along the bottom of casserole dish.
9.  Alternate with layers of banana slices and pudding, ending with pudding on top.
10. Bake for 10 minutes at 350 degrees.

**Serves 6**

# BREAD PUDDING

## The INGREDIENTS I need

| | |
|---|---|
| 1-1/2 cups | Bread, crumbled |
| 3 cups | Milk |
| 2 | Eggs, beaten |
| 2/3 cup | Sugar |
| 1 Tbsp. | Butter or Margarine |
| 1 tsp. | Nutmeg |
| 1 tsp. | Cinnamon |

## The EQUIPMENT I need

Bowl
Measuring cup/spoons
Spoon
8" Baking dish

ꚛꚛꚛꚛꚛꚛꚛꚛꚛꚛꚛꚛꚛꚛ **How To Make It** ꚛꚛꚛꚛꚛꚛꚛꚛꚛꚛꚛꚛꚛꚛ

1. Combine bread pieces, milk, eggs, sugar and butter in bowl.
2. Add nutmeg and cinnamon and mix well.
3. Pour into an 8" greased baking dish.
4. Bake at 350 degrees for 35 minutes until firm.

**Serves 4**

# CORN PUDDING

## The INGREDIENTS I need

| | |
|---|---|
| 1 can | Cream Style Corn |
| 1 cup | Milk |
| 1 Tbsp. | Butter or Margarine |
| 1 Tbsp. | Sugar |
| 3 | Eggs, separated |

## The EQUIPMENT I need

Pan
Measuring cup/spoons
Egg beater
Casserole Pan
Bowl

## ৪৪৪৪৪৪৪৪৪৪৪৪৪৪৪৪ How To Make It ৪৪৪৪৪৪৪৪৪৪৪৪৪৪৪৪

1. Boil the corn and milk together.
2. Stir in the butter or margarine, sugar and beaten egg yolks.
3. Beat egg whites until stiff.
4. Fold into the corn mixture.
5. Pour into greased casserole pan.
6. Bake uncovered in a 350 degree oven for about 30 minutes.

Serves 6

# RICE PUDDING

## The INGREDIENTS I need

| | |
|---|---|
| 4 | Eggs |
| 2 cups | Milk |
| 1/2 cup | Sugar |
| 1 tsp. | Vanilla |
| 1/2 tsp. | Salt |
| 2 cups | Rice (cooked) |
| 1/2 cup | Raisins |
| 1 tsp. | Cinnamon |
| 1 tsp. | Nutmeg |

## The EQUIPMENT I need

Bowl
Measuring cups
Measuring spoons
Egg beater
Baking dish

## How To Make It

1. Beat eggs, milk, sugar, vanilla and salt.
2. Stir in rice and raisins.
3. Pour mixture into buttered baking dish.
4. Sprinkle with cinnamon and nutmeg.
5. Bake at 325 degrees for 35 minutes.

Serves 4

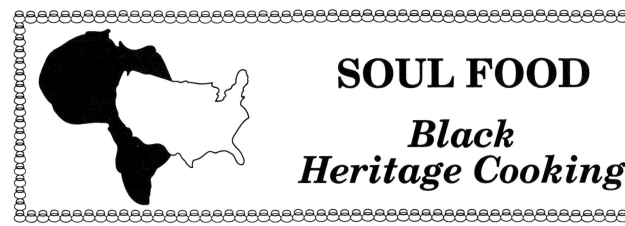

# SOUL FOOD

## *Black Heritage Cooking*

Chitlins/Pig's Feet

Hoppin' John

Collard Greens with
Ham Hocks

Black-eyed Peas

Sweet Potato Pie

Cornbread

Fried Chicken

Macaroni and Cheese

Smothered Cabbage

Biscuits

Peach Cobbler

Smothered Pork Chops
with Gravy

Mustard and Turnip
Greens with Neckbones

Red Beans and Rice

Pound Cake

Fried Fish

Potato Salad

Hush Puppies

Banana Pudding

Neckbones

Red Beans and Rice

Hot Water Cornbread

Apple Brown Betty

# BLACK-EYED PEAS

## The INGREDIENTS I need

1 cup — Dried Black-eyed Peas
1/4 pound — Bacon Ends or lean Salt Pork, diced
1 large — Onion, chopped
1/2 tsp. — Salt
1/4 tsp. — Black Pepper

## The EQUIPMENT I need

Pot/lid
Cutting board/knife
Measuring cup/spoons

## ᵇᵇᵇᵇᵇᵇᵇᵇᵇᵇᵇᵇᵇᵇᵇ How To Make It ᵇᵇᵇᵇᵇᵇᵇᵇᵇᵇᵇᵇᵇᵇᵇᵇ

1. Soak the peas overnight in water to cover; or, boil in water to cover for 3 minutes, then let stand for 1 hour.
2. Parboil bacon or salt pork for 30 minutes.
3. Drain the peas and add to meat.
4. Add onion.
5. Cover and simmer for 1 hour or until peas are done. Add salt and pepper to taste.

Serves 4-6

# CHITTERLINGS (Chitlin's)

## The INGREDIENTS I need

| | |
|---|---|
| 5 pounds | Frozen Chitterlings, thawed |
| 5 cups | Water |
| 2 stalks | Celery with Leaves |
| 2 large | Onions, chopped |
| 2 | Bay Leaves |
| 1 clove | Garlic, minced |
| 1/2 cup | Vinegar |
| 1 tsp. | Salt |
| 1/2 tsp. | Pepper |
| 2 | Red Pepper Pods, cut in pieces (optional) |

## The EQUIPMENT I need

Large pot/lid
Measuring cup/spoons
Cutting board/knife

## ᪏᪏᪏᪏᪏᪏᪏᪏᪏᪏᪏᪏᪏᪏ How To Make It ᪏᪏᪏᪏᪏᪏᪏᪏᪏᪏᪏᪏᪏᪏

1. Soak Chitterlings in cold water to cover for at least 6 hours. Drain.
2. Strip as much fat as possible from each piece and wash thoroughly in cold water. Make sure it is entirely free of dirt.
3. Cut into small pieces about 1 inch.
4. Place in full pot of water with salt and pepper.
5. Add all other ingredients to the pot and cover.
6. Cook over medium heat until tender about 2-1/2 or 3 hours.
7. Serve with vinegar or hot sauce.

**Serves 4-6**

# HOPPIN' JOHN

## The INGREDIENTS I need

| | |
|---|---|
| 3 Cups | Water |
| 1 cup | Black-eyed Peas |
| 1/4 pound | Salt Pork, Bacon or Ham ends, Ham Hock or Smoked Turkey pieces |
| 1 medium | Onion, chopped |
| 1 | Bay Leaf |
| 1/2 tsp. | Salt |
| 1/4 tsp. | Pepper |
| Pinch | Cayenne Pepper |
| 1 cup | Rice, uncooked |

## The EQUIPMENT I need

Pot/lid
Saucepan/lid
Measuring cup/spoons
Cutting board/knife

## 88888888888888 How To Make It 8888888888888

1. Combine water and black-eyed peas in large pot. Boil for 30 minutes.
2. Add meat, onions, bay leaf, salt, pepper and cayenne pepper to the pot; simmer for 1 hour.
3. Drain peas.
4. Cook rice separately until it is dry and flaky (30 minutes).
5. Gently stir rice into pot of peas and cook over low heat until all liquid is absorbed.

Serves 4-6

# PIG'S FEET

## The INGREDIENTS I need

| | |
|---|---|
| 5 cups | Water |
| 4 | Pig's Feet, split |
| 1/4 cup | Vinegar, cider |
| 2 medium | Onions, chopped |
| 1 | Garlic clove, split |
| 1 | Bay Leaf |
| 1 tsp. | Salt |
| 1/4 tsp. | Pepper |
| 2 stalks | Celery and Leaves, chopped |

## The EQUIPMENT I need

Large pot/lid
Measuring cup/spoons
Cutting board/knife

ⴲⴲⴲⴲⴲⴲⴲⴲⴲⴲⴲⴲⴲⴲⴲⴲ **How To Make It** ⴲⴲⴲⴲⴲⴲⴲⴲⴲⴲⴲⴲⴲⴲⴲⴲ

1. Clean pig's feet thoroughly.
2. Place all ingredients in a pot.
3. Cover with water. Bring to a boil. Lower heat.
4. Cover pot. Simmer over low heat for 2 hours, or until meat fall off the bones.

Serves 2-4

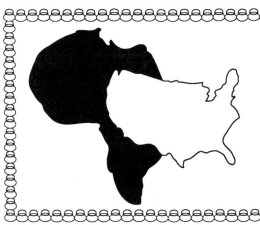

# NEW SOUL FOOD

## *Healthier Old Favorites*

Oven Fried Catfish
Coleslaw
Southern Succotash
Rice Pudding
Baked Hush Puppies

Chicken in the Oven
Collard Greens
Potato Salad
Sweet Potato Pie


Short Ribs
Marinated Green Beans
Red Beans and Rice
Citrus Iced Tea


Sweet Potato Bread
Collard Green Quiche
Grits Souffle
Potato Salad Vinaigrette

# OVEN-FRIED CATFISH

## The INGREDIENTS I need

| | |
|---|---|
| 4 | Catfish Fillets |
| 1/4 cup | Yellow Cornmeal |
| 1/4 cup | Bread Crumbs, dry |
| 1/4 tsp. | Salt |
| 1/4 tsp. | Paprika |
| 1/4 tsp. | Pepper |
| 1/8 tsp. | Garlic Powder |
| 1/8 tsp. | Lowfat Milk |
| 1/2 cup | Margarine, melted |
| | Vegetable Oil Cooking Spray |

## The EQUIPMENT I need

Pan
Bowl
Measuring cup/spoons

8888888888888888 **How To Make It** 8888888888888888

1. Heat oven to 450 degrees.
2. Mix all to dry ingredients together.
3. Dip fish into milk and coat with cornmeal mixture.
4. Spray pan with Pam.
5. Place fish in the pan.
6. Pour melted margarine over fish.
7. Bake for 15 minutes.

**Serves 4**

# COLESLAW

## The INGREDIENTS I need

| | |
|---|---|
| 1 small | Cabbage, shredded |
| 1/2 small | Red Cabbage, shredded |
| 1 cup | Carrots, shredded |
| 1/2 tsp. | Salt (optional) |
| 1/4 tsp. | Pepper |
| 1 cup | Yogurt, plain |
| 1/2 cup | Mayonnaise |
| 4 tsp. | Cider Vinegar |

## The EQUIPMENT I need

Bowl
Measuring cup/spoons
Grater

## ⴲⴲⴲⴲⴲⴲⴲⴲⴲⴲⴲⴲⴲⴲⴲ How To Make It ⴲⴲⴲⴲⴲⴲⴲⴲⴲⴲⴲⴲⴲⴲⴲ

1. Mix yogurt, mayonnaise, vinegar, salt and pepper in a bowl.
2. Grate cabbage, red cabbage an carrots.
3. Pour yogurt mixture over vegetables. Toss well. Cover and chill 4 hours.

**Serves 6**

# SOUTHERN SUCCOTASH

## The INGREDIENTS I need

| | |
|---|---|
| 1 pkg. | Lima Beans, frozen |
| 1 pkg. | Kernel Corn, frozen or canned |
| 1 16-oz. can | Tomatoes |
| 1/2 cup | Onions, chopped |
| 2 Tbsp. | Margarine |
| 1/8 tsp. | Salt |
| 1/4 tsp. | Pepper |
| 1 pkg. | Okra, frozen cut |

## The EQUIPMENT I need

Saucepan
Measuring cup/spoons
Wooden spoon
Cutting board/knife

8888888888888888 **How To Make It** 8888888888888888

1. Combine lima beans, corn, tomato, onion, margarine, salt and pepper in saucepan.
2. Bring to a boil, reduce heat and simmer 20 minutes.
3. Add okra and cook 10 minutes.

**Serves 6**

# RICE PUDDING

## The INGREDIENTS I need

2-1/2 cups Water
3/4 cup Rice
1/2 tsp. Salt
6 Egg Whites
3 cups Lowfat Milk
1/2 cup Sugar
1-1/2 tsp. Lemon Juice
1/2 cup Raisins
1/4 tsp. Nutmeg
1/2 tsp. Cinnamon
Vegetable Oil spray

## The EQUIPMENT I need

Pot
2-quart casserole pan
Measuring cup/spoons
Wooden spoon
Bowl

## ଷଷଷଷଷଷଷଷଷଷଷଷଷଷ How To Make It ଷଷଷଷଷଷଷଷଷଷଷଷଷଷ

1. Bring water to boil in saucepan.
2. Stir in rice and salt.
3. Cover and cook over low heat until all water is absorbed, about 30 minutes.
4. Beat eggs in large bowl.
5. Add remaining ingredients, stir until well blended.
6. Stir in cooked rice.  Pour into casserole sprayed with vegetable oil.
7. Set casserole in a large pan and add 1-inch hot water to pan.
8. Bake uncovered at 350 degrees for 30 minutes; stir.
9. Continue baking until center comes out clean, (about 1 hour).

Serves 6-8

# BAKED HUSH PUPPIES

## The INGREDIENTS I need

| | |
|---|---|
| 2/3 cup | Yellow Cornmeal |
| 1/3 cup | Flour |
| 1 tsp. | Baking Powder |
| 1/8 tsp. | Salt (optional) |
| 1/4 cup | White Onion, minced |
| 1/3 cup | Lowfat Milk |
| 1 Tbsp. | Oil |
| 2 | Egg Whites, beaten |
| | Vegetable Oil Spray |

## The EQUIPMENT I need

Muffin pan
Bowl
Measuring cup/spoons
Wooden spoon

## ᴂᴂᴂᴂᴂᴂᴂᴂᴂᴂᴂᴂᴂᴂᴂᴂ How To Make It ᴂᴂᴂᴂᴂᴂᴂᴂᴂᴂᴂᴂᴂᴂᴂᴂ

1. Combine cornmeal, flour, baking powder and salt in bowl.
2. Add onion, milk, oil and egg whites to dry ingredients.
3. Stir just until moistened.
4. Spray muffin pan with Pam.
5. Spoon batter into muffin pan.
6. Bake at 450 degrees for 10 minutes, until browned.

**Makes 12**

# CHICKEN IN THE OVEN

## The INGREDIENTS I need

| | |
|---|---|
| 2-3 pounds | Chicken |
| 1/2 cup | Flour |
| 1/4 tsp. | Salt |
| 1 tsp. | Paprika |
| 1/4 tsp. | Garlic Powder |
| 1/4 tsp. | Pepper |
| | Cooking spray |

## The EQUIPMENT I need

Pan
Measuring cup/spoons
Fork

ꝏꝏꝏꝏꝏꝏꝏꝏꝏꝏꝏꝏ **How To Make It** ꝏꝏꝏꝏꝏꝏꝏꝏꝏꝏꝏꝏ

1. Coat pan with Pam.
2. Mix flour and seasonings.
3. Coat chicken with flour mixture.
4. Place skin side down in pan.
5. Bake uncovered at 425 degrees for 30 minutes.
6. Turn chicken and cook 30 minutes more.

Serves 6

# COLLARD GREENS

| The INGREDIENTS I need | | The EQUIPMENT I need |
|---|---|---|
| 1 pound | Smoked Turkey Parts | Large saucepan/lid |
| 1-1/2 quarts | Water | Measuring cup/spoons |
| 1 tsp. | Red Pepper, crushed | Cutting board/knife |
| 2 cloves | Garlic, minced | |
| 4 pounds | Collard Greens, fresh or frozen | |
| 1 medium | Onion, chopped | |
| 2 stalks | Celery, chopped | |
| 1 small | Green Pepper, chopped | |
| 1 Tbsp. | Sugar | |
| 1 Tbsp. | Vegetable Oil | |
| 1/8 tsp. | Salt | |
| 1/4 tsp. | Pepper | |

## How To Make It

1. Place turkey in large saucepan.
2. Add water, crushed pepper and garlic.
3. Cover, bring to boil, reduce heat and simmer 30 minutes.
4. Wash leaves thoroughly; chop into bite size pieces.
5. Add collards, onion, celery, green pepper, sugar, oil salt and pepper.
6. Cook 40 minutes or until greens are done.

Serves 8

# POTATO SALAD

## The INGREDIENTS I need

| | |
|---|---|
| 6 medium | Potatoes |
| 1 cup | Light Mayonnaise |
| 1 Tbsp. | Vinegar |
| 1 Tbsp. | Prepared Mustard |
| 1/2 tsp. | Salt (optional) |
| 1/4 tsp. | Pepper |
| 1/2 cup | Celery, chopped |
| 1/4 cup | Pimentos, chopped |
| 1/3 cup | Pickle Relish |
| 4 | Hard-cooked Egg Whites, chopped |

## The EQUIPMENT I need

Pot\lid
Cutting board/knife
Bowl
Measuring cup/spoons
Wooden spoon
Foil

## සසසසසසසසසසසසස How To Make It සසසසසසසසසසසසස

1. Wash potatoes. Leave skin on but remove eyes.
2. Boil water and add potatoes.
3. Cover and heat for 30 minutes; drain.
4. Cool and peel. Cut into cubes.
5. Mix mayonnaise, vinegar, mustard, salt and pepper in bowl.
6. Add potatoes, celery, pimentos and pickle relish. Toss.
7. Stir in eggs.
8. Cover and refrigerate for 4 hours.

**Serves 6-8**

# SWEET POTATO PIE

## The INGREDIENTS I need

| | |
|---|---|
| 4 | Egg Whites |
| 3/4 cup | Sugar |
| 1/4 cup | Orange Juice |
| 1/2 tsp. | Orange Rind |
| 1 tsp. | Cinnamon |
| 1/4 tsp. | Nutmeg |
| 1/2 cup | Lowfat Milk |
| 2 Tbsp. | Margarine, melted |
| 2 cups | Sweet Potatoes, cooked mashed |
| 1 | 9-inch Pie Shell, unbaked |

## The EQUIPMENT I need

Bowl
Electric Mixer
Measuring cup/spoons
Wooden spoon

ᴁᴁᴁᴁᴁᴁᴁᴁᴁᴁᴁᴁᴁᴁᴁᴁ **How To Make It** ᴁᴁᴁᴁᴁᴁᴁᴁᴁᴁᴁᴁᴁᴁᴁᴁ

1. Beat egg whites well.
2. Add sugar, orange juice, orange rind, spices and margarine.
3. Mix thoroughly. Add milk and stir.
4. Add mashed sweet potatoes and mix thoroughly.
5. Turn into pie shell and bake in preheated 350 degree oven for 1 hour or until firm.

**Serves 8**

# SHORT RIBS

## The INGREDIENTS I need

| | |
|---|---|
| 2 pounds | Lean Beef Short ribs |
| 1/2 cup | Tomato Juice |
| 1/2 cup | Tomatoes, crushed |
| 5 | Carrots, sliced |
| 5 medium | Potatoes, diced |
| 3 medium | Onions, chopped |
| 3 | Celery Stalks, cut into pieces |
| 1/4 tsp. | Garlic Powder |
| 1/4 tsp. | Onion Powder |
| 1/8 tsp. | Salt |
| 1/4 tsp. | Pepper |
| 1 | Bay Leaf |
| | Vegetable Oil Spray |

## The EQUIPMENT I need

Skillet/lid
Measuring cup/spoons
Cutting board/knife
Fork
Wooden spoon

## ᵇᵇᵇᵇᵇᵇᵇᵇᵇᵇᵇᵇᵇᵇᵇ How To Make It ᵇᵇᵇᵇᵇᵇᵇᵇᵇᵇᵇᵇᵇᵇᵇ

1. Coat skillet with Pam.
2. Heat skillet, add short ribs and brown on all sides.
3. Add tomato juice and crushed tomatoes.
4. Cover and simmer 1-1/2 hours.
5. Skim off fat; add remaining ingredients.
5. Cover and continue cooking until meat and vegetables are tender, about 1 hour.

Serves 6

# MARINATED GREEN BEANS

## The INGREDIENTS I need

1-1/2 pounds    Fresh Green Beans
 or
1 pkg.          Beans, frozen
1/4 tsp.        Garlic Powder
1/4 tsp.        Ground Ginger
1/4 cup         Orange Juice
1/4 cup         Vegetable Oil
2 tsp.          Lemon Juice
1/4 tsp.        Salt
1 tsp.          Orange Rind, grated
Dash            Cayenne Pepper

## The EQUIPMENT I need

Pot/lid
Measuring cup/spoon
Colander
Container with lid

ꙮꙮꙮꙮꙮꙮꙮꙮꙮꙮꙮꙮꙮꙮꙮ **How To Make It** ꙮꙮꙮꙮꙮꙮꙮꙮꙮꙮꙮꙮꙮꙮꙮ

1. Steam green beans in a saucepan with 1/4 cup water.
2. Cover tightly and heat to boiling;  reduce heat.
3. Steam until crisp 8 to 10 minutes.
4. Rise under cold water;  drain.
5. Shake remaining ingredients in tightly covered container.
   Pour over beans.
6. Cover and refrigerate at least 4 hours, stirring
   occasionally;  drain.

Serves 4-6

# RED BEANS AND RICE

## The INGREDIENTS I need

| | |
|---|---|
| 1/2 pound | Dry Red Beans (soaked overnight) |
| 1/4 pound | Smoked Turkey Links, sliced (optional) |
| 5 cups | Water |
| 1 | Bay Leaf |
| 1/2 tsp. | Thyme Leaves |
| 1 cup | Green Pepper, chopped |
| 1 cup | Onions, chopped |
| 1/2 cup | Celery, chopped |
| 3 cloves | Garlic, minced |
| 1 tsp. | Red Pepper, crushed |
| 1 cup | Rice |

## The EQUIPMENT I need

Large pot
Measuring cup/spoons
Wooden spoon
Cutting board/knife

## How To Make It

1. Drain beans, after soaking overnight, or instead of soaking, cover beans with water, bring to a boil then turn off heat and let stand for one hour.
2. Combine beans, smoked turkey and water in a pot and bring to a boil 30 minutes.
3. Add the remaining ingredients to the pot; reduce heat, simmer uncovered for 1-12 hours or until beans are tender.
4. Add more water if mixture is too thick.
5. Cook rice according to directions.
6. Serve beans over rice.

Serves 6

# CITRUS ICED TEA

## The INGREDIENTS I need

| | |
|---|---|
| 3 cups | Brewed Tea |
| 1 cup | Pineapple Juice |
| 2 tsp. | Lemon Juice |
| 2 Tbsp. | Lime Juice |
| 2 Tbsp. | Sugar |
| | Ice cubes |
| | Mint Leaves (optional) |
| | Orange Rind Strips |

## The EQUIPMENT I need

Teapot
Pitcher
Measuring cup/spoons
Glasses

88888888888888888 **How To Make It** 88888888888888888

1. Boil water and add 2 tea bags.
2. Combine first 5 ingredients in pitcher; stir well.
3. Chill thoroughly.
4. To pour 1/2 cup into ice-filled glasses.
5. Garnish with mint leaf and orange rind strips.

Makes 4 cups

# SWEET POTATO BREAD

## The INGREDIENTS I need

| | |
|---|---|
| 1/3 cup | Shortening or Margarine |
| 1/4 cup | Brown Sugar |
| 2 | Eggs |
| 1/2 cup | Molasses |
| 1 cup | Sweet Potatoes or Yams, cooked, peeled and mashed (may be canned) |
| 2 cups | Wheat or White Flour |
| 1/4 tsp. | Baking Powder |
| 1 Tsp. | Baking Soda |
| 1/2 tsp. | Salt |
| 1/2 tsp. | Cinnamon |
| 1/2 tsp. | Nutmeg |
| 1/2 tsp. | Allspice |
| 1/4 tsp. | Cloves |
| 1/4 cup | Raisins |
| 1/2 cup | Dates, optional |
| 1 cup | Walnuts or Pecans, chopped |
| | Vegetable Oil Spray |

## The EQUIPMENT I need

Loaf pan
Bowl
Electric Mixer
Measuring cup/spoons
Wooden spoon
Sifter

## ᙎᙎᙎᙎᙎᙎᙎᙎᙎᙎᙎᙎ How To Make It ᙎᙎᙎᙎᙎᙎᙎᙎᙎᙎᙎᙎ

1. Preheat oven to 350 degrees.
2. In a large bowl combine shortening or margarine, sugar and eggs.
3. Beat until light and fluffy.
4. Stir in molasses and sweet potatoes or yams.
5. Sift dry ingredients and spices; add to mixture.
6. Add raisins and nuts. Mix well.
7. Bake 1 hour in a greased loaf pan.

**Serves 5-10**

# COLLARD GREEN QUICHE

## The INGREDIENTS I need

| | |
|---|---|
| 4 | Eggs |
| 1 cup | Half-and-Half |
| 1/2 tsp. | Salt |
| 1/4 tsp. | Pepper |
| 1/4 tsp. | Oregano |
| 1/2 tsp. | Onion Powder |
| 1/4 cup | Green Onions, chopped |
| 1/4 cup | Green Pepper, chopped |
| 1/4 cup | Mushrooms, chopped (fresh or canned) |
| 3 cups | Collard Greens, cooked, chopped (fresh or frozen) |
| 1 cup | Cheddar Cheese, grated |
| 1 cup | Mozzarella Cheese, grated |
| 1 9-inch | Pie Crust, frozen or homemade |

## The EQUIPMENT I need

Pie pan
Measuring cup/spoons
Cutting board/knife
Grater
Bowl
Fork
Wooden spoon

## ᵦᵦᵦᵦᵦᵦᵦᵦᵦᵦᵦ How To Make It ᵦᵦᵦᵦᵦᵦᵦᵦᵦᵦᵦ

1. Preheat oven to 350 degrees.
2. Cook pie crust for 10 minutes.
3. Beat eggs and half-and-half in a bowl.
4. Add salt, pepper, oregano, onion powder, green onions, onions, mushroom and collard greens; set aside.
5. Mix cheeses together in bowl.
6. Sprinkle half of cheese mixture onto pie crust.
7. Pour egg mixture on top of cheese.
8. Sprinkle remaining cheese on top.
9. Bake for 1 hour.

**Serves 8**

# GRITS SOUFFLE

## The INGREDIENTS I need

| | |
|---|---|
| 4 | Eggs, separated |
| 3/4 cup | Lowfat Milk |
| 1/3 tsp. | Salt |
| 1/4 tsp. | White Pepper |
| 1-1/2 cups | Grits, cooked |
| 8 oz. | Cream Cheese, softened |
| 2 cups | Sharp Cheddar Cheese, grated |

## The EQUIPMENT I need

Casserole pan
Electric mixer
Grater
Bowl
Measuring cup/spoons
Wooden spoon

8888888888888888 **How To Make It** 8888888888888888

1. Preheat oven to 350 degrees.
2. Beat egg whites until stiff peaks form.
3. Beat egg yolks, milk, salt and pepper.
4. Add grits and creams cheese to milk and egg mixture. Beat until smooth.
5. Fold in 1 cup of cheese and egg whites.
6. Pour into greased casserole dish.
7. Sprinkle 1 cup of cheese on top.
8. Bake for 45 minutes until firm.

**Serves 8-10**

# POTATO SALAD VINAIGRETTE

## The INGREDIENTS I need

| | |
|---|---|
| 3 cups | Water |
| 2 pounds | Red Potatoes |
| 1/3 cup | White Vinegar |
| 1/3 cup | Olive Oil |
| 2 T. | Red Wine Vinegar or Balsamic Vinegar |
| 1 tsp. | Dijon Mustard |
| 1/4 tsp. | Salt |
| 1/4 tsp. | Pepper |
| 2 cloves | Garlic, minced |
| 6 slices | Beef or Turkey Bacon |
| 1/4 cup | Parsley, (fresh or dried), minced |
| 1 head | Lettuce |

## The EQUIPMENT I need

Pot
Cutting board/knife
Measuring cup/spoon
Collander
Bowl
Platter

## ᙁᙁᙁᙁᙁᙁᙁᙁᙁᙁᙁᙁᙁᙁᙁ How To Make It ᙁᙁᙁᙁᙁᙁᙁᙁᙁᙁᙁᙁᙁᙁᙁ

1. Boil water, add potatoes and cook for 20 minutes.
2. Drain potatoes, rinse with cold water.
3. Dry with paper towel. Cover and refrigerate about 1 hour.
4. Cut potatoes into quarters or cubes.
5. Sprinkle white vinegar over potatoes. Cover and set aside.
6. Mix olive oil, red wine vinegar, mustard, salt, pepper, garlic and parsley in bowl.
7. Cook bacon until crisp, drain and crumble.
8. Before serving, pour dressing over potatoes.
9. Place potato salad on a bed of lettuce and add crumbled bacon on top.

**Serves 4-6**

- - - - - - - - - - - - - - - *HEALTHIER WAYS TO FIX OLD FAVORITES*

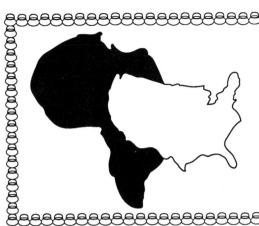

# AFRICAN COOKING

## *Recipes from the Motherland*

African Chicken and Greens
African Health Salad
African Slush Punch
Akara
Chicken in Groundnut Sauce
Cousocous
Dun Dun (Fried Yam Slices)
Fufu
Jollof Rice
Peanut Soup
Shoko (Festival Stew)
Yam Fritters

# AFRICAN CHICKEN AND GREENS

## The INGREDIENTS I need

| | |
|---|---|
| 6 pieces | Chicken |
| 1 medium | Onion, chopped |
| 1 | carrot, sliced |
| 1 clove | Garlic, chopped |
| 1/2 tsp. | Ground Coriander |
| 1 Tbsp. | Butter or Margarine |
| 1 pkg. 10-oz. | Spinach or Collard Greens, frozen |
| | Salt to taste |

## The EQUIPMENT I need

Pot
Measuring cup/spoons
Wooden spoon
Skillet

## ஐஐஐஐஐஐஐஐஐஐஐஐஐ How To Make It ஐஐஐஐஐஐஐஐஐஐஐஐஐ

1. Add 1 cup of water to pot.
2. Add chicken, onion and carrots.
3. Cover and simmer 1 hour until tender.
4. Remove chicken to cool.
5. Save onions and carrots, throw out stock.
6. Melt butter in skillet; add salt, garlic and coriander.
7. Brown chicken on all sides.
8. Add greens (thawed) to skillet.
9. Cover and cook 15-25 minutes.
10. Serve with rice.

**Serves 4-6**

# AFRICAN HEALTH SALAD

## The INGREDIENTS I need

| | |
|---|---|
| 1 head | Green Lettuce |
| 1 head | Cabbage |
| 1/2 head | Red Cabbage |
| 1 bunch | Spinach |
| 1 cup | Carrots, grated |
| 1cup | Beets, grated |
| 1/2 cup | Raisins |
| 1/2 cup | Sun flower Seeds |
| 1/2 | Broccoli |
| 1/2 | Cauliflower |
| 1/2 cup | Bean Sprouts |
| 1cup | Alfalfa |
| 1/2 cup | Celery, diced |
| Tofu | (Optional) |

## The EQUIPMENT I need

Grater
Knife/cutting board
Salad spinner
Paper towel
Wooden salad bowl

## ᎧᎧᎧᎧᎧᎧᎧᎧᎧᎧᎧᎧᎧ How To Make It ᎧᎧᎧᎧᎧᎧᎧᎧᎧᎧᎧᎧᎧ

1. Wash and dry all vegetables.
2. Put all the ingredients into salad bowl.
3. Toss it with your favorite dressing.

**Serves 8-10**

# AFRICAN SLUSH PUNCH

## The INGREDIENTS I need

| | |
|---|---|
| 4 cups | Sugar |
| 6 cups | Water |
| 1 12-oz. can | Frozen Orange Juice |
| 6-oz. can | Frozen Lemonade |
| 6-oz. can | Water |
| 1 large can | Unsweetened Pineapple Juice |
| 5 mashed | Bananas |
| 3 qts. | Gingerale |

## The EQUIPMENT I need

Wooden spoon
Measuring Cup
Can Opener
Sauce pan
Blender
Large Container

## ꙮꙮꙮꙮꙮꙮꙮꙮꙮ How To Make It ꙮꙮꙮꙮꙮꙮꙮꙮꙮ

1. Boil sugar and 6 cups water in a large saucepan for 3 minutes. Cool.
2. Mash bananas in blender and combine in large container with fruit juices and the 6-ounce can water.
3. Add sugar mixture and blend well.
4. Freeze for at least 24 hours.
5. Remove from freezer one hour before serving. Mash to a pulp.
6. Add gingerale, mix and serve.

Serves 8-10

# AKARA (Nigeria)

## The INGREDIENTS I need

| | |
|---|---|
| 1 cup | Black-eyed Peas, Navy or Lima Beans cooked |
| 1/2 cup | Meat (any kind), cooked, chopped fine |
| 1/2 cup | Onions, chopped |
| 1/2 tsp. | Salt |
| 1/4 tsp. | Pepper |
| 1/4 tsp. | Ground Red Chili Pepper |
| 1 | Egg |
| | Peanut oil for frying |

## The EQUIPMENT I need

Skillet
Fork
Measuring cup/spoons
Bowl
Cutting board/knife
Paper towel

## ᬊᬊᬊᬊᬊᬊᬊᬊᬊᬊᬊᬊᬊᬊᬊᬊ How To Make It ᬊᬊᬊᬊᬊᬊᬊᬊᬊᬊᬊᬊᬊᬊᬊᬊ

1. Mash beans with a fork.
2. Add all the ingredients.
3. Form into small balls.
4. Coat lightly with flour.
5. Fry in oil until crisp and brown.
6. Drain on paper towel.

**Serves 3-4**

# CHICKEN IN GROUNDNUT SAUCE

## The INGREDIENTS I need

| | |
|---|---|
| 2 Tbsp. | Peanut Oil |
| 3 pounds | Chicken, cut up |
| 1/4 cup | Dried Shrimp |
| 1 cup | Hot Water |
| 2 Tbsp. | Tomato Paste |
| 1 14-1/2 oz. can | Stewed Tomatoes |
| 2 medium | Onions, chopped |
| 3 cloves | Garlic, chopped |
| 1 tsp. | Cayenne Pepper |
| 1/4 tsp. | Ground Ginger |
| 2 | Bay Leaves |
| 2 tsp. | Chili Powder |
| 1 cup | Crunch Peanut Butter |

## The EQUIPMENT I need

Pot/lid
Cutting board/knife
Skillet
Measuring cup/spoons
Wooden spoon
Colander

## 8888888888888888 How To Make It 8888888888888888

1. Heat oil in skillet. Cook chicken over medium heat until brown on all sides. 15 minutes.
2. Remove chicken, drain fat from skillet.
3. Heat dried shrimp, water, bring tomato paste, tomatoes, onions and seasonings to boiling in pot; reduce heat.
4. Cover and simmer 10 minutes. Add chicken, cover and simmer 45 minutes.
5. Stir some of the hot liquid into peanut butter, stir into chicken mixture.
6. Turn chicken to coat with sauce.
7. Cover and cook until chicken is done, about 10-15 minutes.
8. Serve over rice.

**Serves 6**

# COUSCOUS

## The INGREDIENTS I need

| | |
|---|---|
| 1-1/2 pounds | Boneless Lamb cut into 1-1/2 inch cubes |
| 1 envelope | Onion Soup Mix |
| 1 tsp. | Salt |
| 1/4 tsp. | Pepper |
| 1/4 tsp. | Ginger |
| Dash | Cayenne |
| 3-1/2 cups | Boiling Water |
| 2 Tbsp. | Corn Oil |
| 1 | Broiler-Fryer chicken, cut up |
| 4 medium | Carrots, pared and cut into pieces |
| 2 medium | White Turnips, pared and cut into pieces |
| 2 medium | Zucchini, cut into pieces |
| 6 servings | Cooked Farina or Rice |

## The EQUIPMENT I need

Pot/cover
Skillet
Measuring cup/spoons
Wooden spoon
Cutting board/knife

## ꠸꠸꠸꠸꠸꠸꠸꠸꠸꠸꠸꠸꠸ How To Make It ꠸꠸꠸꠸꠸꠸꠸꠸꠸꠸꠸꠸꠸

1. Brown lamb pieces on all sides in large saucepan over low heat.
2. Stir in soup mix, salt, pepper, ginger, cayenne and boiling water.
3. Heat corn oil in large skillet.
4. Add chicken, brown lightly on all sides over low heat.
5. Add chicken and turnips to simmered lamb; cover and simmer 15 minutes.
6. Add carrots and zucchini to simmered meat and vegetables.
7. Arrange serving platter with farina or rice, meat and vegetables.

Makes 6 servings

# DUN DUN (Fried Yam Slices)

## The INGREDIENTS I need

## The EQUIPMENT I need

| | | |
|---|---|---|
| 6 medium | Yams or Sweet Potatoes | Cutting board/knife |
| Water | | Measuring cup/spoons |
| 1 tsp. | Salt | Skillet/Pot |
| 1 cup | Flour, seasoned with | Tongs |
| | 1 tsp. each of salt and pepper | |
| 2 | Eggs, beaten with 2 Tbsp. water | |
| | Oil for frying | |

## ꙮꙮꙮꙮꙮꙮꙮꙮꙮꙮ How To Make It ꙮꙮꙮꙮꙮꙮꙮꙮꙮꙮ

1. Peel and cut potatoes into 1/2 inch slices.
2. Boil slices in salted water until tender.
3. Drain.
4. Put seasoned flour into one bowl.
5. Put egg mixture into another bowl.
6. Dip slices first in flour, then egg and flour again.
7. Fry until golden brown on both sides.

# FUFU

## The INGREDIENTS I need

1 large  Yam
1         Egg
5 Tbsp.  Evaporated Milk
1 small  Onion, grated
3 Tbsp.  Butter or Margarine
Pinch   Garlic Salt

## The EQUIPMENT I need

Pot
Skillet
Measuring cup/spoons
Cutting board/knife
Bowl
Wooden spoon

ꙮꙮꙮꙮꙮꙮꙮꙮꙮꙮꙮꙮꙮ **How To Make It** ꙮꙮꙮꙮꙮꙮꙮꙮꙮꙮꙮꙮꙮ

1. Peel and cut yam into small pieces.
2. Boil pieces until tender in 1/2 cup water for 20 minutes.
3. Drain off the water and mash until smooth.
4. Add the egg, milk, onion and garlic salt.
5. Beat and roll into 2" balls. (If the mixture is too wet add a little flour.
6. Fry in butter or margarine until brown.

**Serves 2-3**

# JOLLOF RICE (West Africa)

## The INGREDIENTS I need

| | |
|---|---|
| 1/2 cup | Smoked Ham, small diced, (optional) |
| 4-6 | Chicken pieces |
| 1/2 tsp. | Salt |
| 1/4 tsp. | Pepper |
| 4 Tbsp. | Peanut Oil |
| 1 | Onion, chopped |
| 2 cubed | Chicken Bouillon |
| 1/8 tsp. | Red Pepper |
| 1/2 tsp. | Thyme |
| 1-1/2 cups | Water |
| 1 clove | Garlic, chopped |
| 1 6 oz. can | Tomato Paste |
| 2 large ripe | Tomatoes, peeled and chopped |
| 1-1/2 cups | Rice, uncooked |
| 1/2 cup | Green Peas (Canned or frozen) |
| 1/2 cup | String Beans (Canned or frozen) |
| 1/2 cup | Carrots |
| 1/2 cup | Green Pepper |

## The EQUIPMENT I need

Frying pan
Large pot/lid
Measuring cup/spoons
Cutting board/knife
Can Opener

## 8888888888888888 How To Make It 8888888888888888

1. Season chicken with salt and black pepper.
2. Place oil in frying pan and heat for 5 minutes.
3. Add chicken and brown on both sides.
4. Place chicken in pot.
5. Add onions, garlic and smoked ham in frying pan and saute.
6. Add bouillon cubes, red pepper, thyme, tomato paste and 1-1/2 cups water to pot and stir well.
7. Simmer for 10 minutes; add rice and vegetables to pot.
8. Stir well and cover. Cook on low heat for 40 minutes.

**Serves 4-6**

# PEANUT SOUP (Ghana Groundnut Soup)

## The INGREDIENTS I need

| 1 | Chicken, cut up |
| 1 medium | Onion, chopped |
| 1 can | Tomatoes |
| 1 cup | Peanut Butter |
| | Water |
| | Red Pepper to taste (optional) |

## The EQUIPMENT I need

Large saucepan
Cutting board/knife
Measuring cup

8888888888888888 How To Make It 8888888888888888

1. Brown chicken and onions in large saucepan until golden.
2. Add cold water to cover chicken.
3. Add tomatoes and salt to taste.
4. Bring to boil; lower heat and simmer for 15 minutes.
5. Mix the peanut butter into a smooth cream with some of the hot stock.
6. Pour this creamed paste into the saucepan.
7. Cook slowly until the oil rises to the top of the soup.

Serves 6

# SHOKO (Festival Stew)

## The INGREDIENTS I need

| | |
|---|---|
| 2 pounds | Boneless Stew Beef, cubed |
| 1/2 cup | Peanut Oil |
| 4 | Tomatoes, chopped |
| 3 medium | Onions, chopped |
| 1/2 tsp. | Green Chili Peppers |
| 1/2 tsp. | Red Chili Peppers |
| 1 tsp. | Salt |
| 1 cup | Water |
| 1 pound | Spinach Leaves, fresh cut into small pieces. |

## The EQUIPMENT I need

Skillet
Measuring cup/spoons
Cutting board/knife
Wooden spoon

## 88888888888888888 How To Make It 888888888888888888

1. Brown meat in oil in skillet.
2. Add water and simmer until tender.
3. Add chili peppers and salt.
4. Add tomatoes and onions.
5. Cook until vegetables are tender.
6. Wash spinach thoroughly in cold water.
7. Add spinach and cook until just tender.

**Serves 4-6**

# YAM FRITTERS

## The INGREDIENTS I need

1-1/2 pounds Yam
1            Egg, beaten
1/2 tsp.    Salt
1/4 tsp.    Pepper
1/4 tsp.    Thyme
1/8 tsp.    Cayenne Pepper or
             Red Pepper
1/2           Green Chili, seeded
             and minced
1 medium   Onion, chopped
1 medium   Tomato, chopped
1/2 cup     Bread Crumbs
             Peanut Oil for frying

## The EQUIPMENT I need

Pot
Skillet
Cutting board/knife
Measuring cup/spoons
Bowl

## ෂෂෂෂෂෂෂෂෂෂෂෂෂ How To Make It ෂෂෂෂෂෂෂෂෂෂෂෂෂ

1. Boil yams with skin until tender.
2. Peel and mash smooth.
3. Saute chopped onion, tomato and chili pepper in 2 tablespoons oil until brown.
4. Add seasonings and sauteed mixture to yams.
5. Add beaten egg and bread crumbs and mix well.
6. Form into small patties and saute in peanut oil until brown on both sides.

**Serves 4-6**

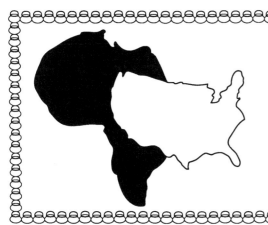

# CARIBBEAN COOKING
## *Island Treasures*

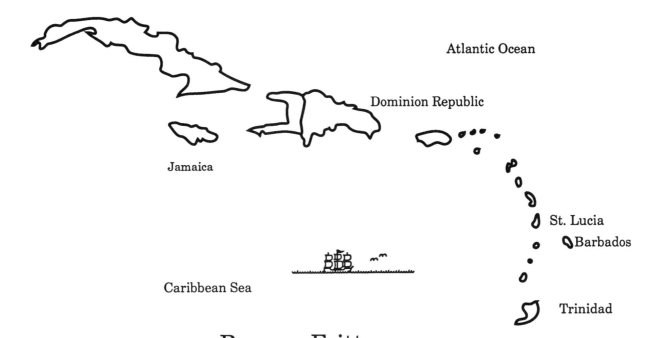

Atlantic Ocean

Dominion Republic

Jamaica

St. Lucia

Barbados

Caribbean Sea

Trinidad

Banana Fritters
Callaloo
Curried Lamb
Fried Plantains
Ginger Beer
Jamaican Beef Patties (with Pastry recipe)
Jerk Chicken
Peanut Punch
Rice and Peas

# BANANA FRITTERS

## The INGREDIENTS I need

| | |
|---|---|
| 2 large | Bananas, ripe, mashed |
| 3 Tbsp. | Flour |
| 1/2 tsp. | Baking Powder |
| 2 Tbsp. | Sugar |
| 1 | Egg, beaten |
| Dash | Cinnamon |
| | Confectioner's Sugar (Powdered) |
| | Oil for frying |

## The EQUIPMENT I need

Bowl
Fork
Measuring cup/spoons
Skillet

## ᗧᗧᗧᗧᗧᗧᗧᗧᗧᗧᗧᗧᗧᗧᗧ How To Make It ᗧᗧᗧᗧᗧᗧᗧᗧᗧᗧᗧᗧᗧᗧᗧ

1. In a bowl, mash the bananas well.
2. Add flour, baking powder, sugar egg and cinnamon. Stir well.
3. Preheat oil in frying pan.
4. Carefully drop tablespoons of dough into oil.
5. Fry for 2 or 3 minutes, until golden brown.
6. Remove fritters from oil.
7. Drain on paper towels.
8. Sprinkle with powdered sugar. Serve immediately.

**Makes 12 fritters**

# CALLALOO SOUP

## The INGREDIENTS I need

| | |
|---|---|
| 1 large | Onion, chopped |
| 3 cloves | Garlic, minced |
| 4 T. | Butter or Margarine |
| 1 pound | Spinach (fresh) or Callaloo, chopped |
| 3 cups | Chicken Broth |
| 1/2 cup | Coconut Milk |
| 1 T. | Salt |
| 1-1/2 T. | Black Pepper |
| 1/2 pound | Crabmeat, (fresh, canned, or frozen), cooked |
| Dash | Pepper Sauce to taste |

## The EQUIPMENT I need

Skillet
Cutting board/knife
Measuring cup/spoon
Wooden spoon
Paper towel

## ၆၆၆၆၆၆၆၆၆၆၆၆၆၆ How To Make It ၆၆၆၆၆၆၆၆၆၆၆၆၆၆

1. Wash and rinse the spinach or callaloo thoroughly.
2. Pat dry with paper towels. Remove stems.
3. Sauté the onions and garlic in a skillet for 5 minutes.
4. Add all of the ingredients except the crabmeat. Bring to a boil, then simmer gently for 30 minutes.
5. Add crabmeat and stir well. Cook for another 5 minutes until cooked.

Serves 4-6

# CURRIED LAMB

## The INGREDIENTS I need

| | |
|---|---|
| 1 pound | Lamb of Goat, cubed |
| 1 tsp. | Salt |
| 1 tsp. | Black Pepper |
| 2 cloves | Garlic, chopped |
| 2 Tbsp. | Curry Powder |
| 1 | Chili, seeded and diced |
| 1 medium | Onion, chopped |
| 2 | Green Onions, chopped |
| 2 Tbsp. | Oil |
| 2 cups | Water, hot |
| 2 medium | Potatoes, diced |

## The EQUIPMENT I need

Bowl
Frying pan
Cutting board/knife
Measuring cup/spoons
Wooden spoon

## 88888888888888888 How To Make It 88888888888888888

1. Place meat in a bowl and rub with salt, pepper, garlic, curry powder, chili, onions and green onions.
2. Cover and place in refrigerate for 2 hours or overnight.
3. In a frying pan, heat oil over medium heat for 1 minute.
4. Brown meat.
5. Add water and seasoning and stir; cover and cook for 1 hour.
6. Add potatoes; stir well and cook for 20 minutes.
7. Serve with rice.

**Serves 4**

# FRIED PLANTAINS

## The INGREDIENTS I need

2 ripe    Plantains, (black)
1/4 cup    Vegetable Oil

## The EQUIPMENT I need

Skillet
Measuring cup
Knife
Fork
Paper towel

### ᠖᠖᠖᠖᠖᠖᠖᠖᠖᠖᠖᠖᠖᠖ How To Make It ᠖᠖᠖᠖᠖᠖᠖᠖᠖᠖᠖᠖᠖᠖

1. Cut plantains in half.
2. Peel them and cut again in half but horizontally.
3. Pour oil into skillet.
4. Place plantain into skillet.
5. Cook until golden brown in color.
6. Place on paper towel to absorb the oil.
7. Sprinkle with sugar, brown sugar or powdered sugar.

**Serves 2-4**

# GINGER BEER

## The INGREDIENTS I need

| | |
|---|---|
| 3/4 cup | Ginger Root, grated |
| 6 cups | Boiling Water |
| 2 Tbsp. | Lime Juice |
| 1-1/2 cups | Sugar |
| 1/2 tsp. | Dried Yeast |

## The EQUIPMENT I need

Grater
Measuring cup/spoons
Tea Kettle
Container with lid
Glass

## &&&&&&&&&&&&&&&& How To Make It &&&&&&&&&&&&&&&&

1. Combine all the ingredients.
2. Stir well and place in a large container.
3. Seal tightly and leave at room temperature for 24 hours.
4. Strain and refrigerate until chilled.

Makes 2 quarts

# JAMAICAN BEEF PATTIES

## The INGREDIENTS I need

1 pound Ground Beef or Turkey
1          Onion, chopped
1 Tbsp.  Celery, chopped
2 Green Onions, chopped
2 Tbsp.  Butter or Margarine
1 clove  Garlic, crushed
1/4 tsp.  Garlic Powder
1/4 cup  Tomato Paste or
            4 tomatoes, peeled and
            chopped
1/4 tsp.  Tumeric
1/4 tsp.  Cumin
1/4 tsp.  Ginger
1/8 tsp.  Coriander
1/8 tsp.  Cinnamon
Salt and Pepper to taste

## The EQUIPMENT I need

Skillet
Measuring cup/spoons
Cutting board/knife
Wooden spoon
Rolling pin
Saucer
Pastry brush
Baking sheet

*Pastry recipe for Beef Patties
 in on the following page.

## ᠍᠍᠍᠍᠍᠍᠍᠍᠍᠍᠍᠍᠍᠍᠍ How To Make It ᠍᠍᠍᠍᠍᠍᠍᠍᠍᠍᠍᠍᠍᠍᠍

1. Heat the oil in a skillet. Add onion, celery, garlic and green onions and saute for 5 minutes.
2. Add meat and cook for 10 minutes.
3. Stir in the rest of the ingredients.
4. Pour 1/2 cup water to mixture and cook on low for 20 minutes. Stir frequently. Let cool.
5. Preheat over to 400 degrees.
6. Roll out the pastry and cut into 12 round, 7 inches in diameter. Use a saucer as a guide.
7. Put 2 tablespoons of filling on one side of each pastry round.
8. Fold over to form a crescent.
9. Crimp the edges with a fork to seal them.
10. Place patties on ungreased baking sheet and brush the top of each with egg yolk.
11. Bake 25-30 minutes until golden brown.

Makes 12-15 patties

# PASTRY FOR BEEF PATTIES

## The INGREDIENTS I need

4 cups    Flour
2 tsp.    Tumeric
1 tsp.    Salt
1 cup     Shortening
3 Tbsp.   Ice Water
2         Egg Yolks

## The EQUIPMENT I need

Bowl
Measuring cup/spoons
Sifter
Plastic wrap
Fork

8888888888888888 **How To Make It** 8888888888888888

1. Sift the flour, tumeric and salt into a bowl.
2. Cut in the shortening and rub in until the mixture resembles coarse meal.
3. Add 3 tablespoons ice water to form a firm dough.
4. Cover the dough with plastic wrap and chill for 2 hours.

# JERK CHICKEN

## The INGREDIENTS I need

| | |
|---|---|
| 1 Tbsp. | Ground Allspice |
| 1 Tbsp. | Dried Thyme |
| 1 tsp. | Cayenne Pepper |
| 1 tsp. | Ground Black Pepper |
| 1/2 tsp. | Nutmeg |
| 1/2 tsp. | Cinnamon |
| 1 tsp. | Salt |
| 2 Tbsp. | Garlic Powder |
| 1 Tbsp. | Sugar |
| 1/4 cup | Olive Oil |
| 1/4 cup | Soy Sauce |
| 3/4 cup | White Vinegar |
| 1/2 cup | Orange Juice (optional) |
| Juice | 1 Lime (optional) |
| 1 cup | White Onion, chopped |
| 3 | Green Onions, chopped fine |
| 4 | Chicken Breasts, trimmed of fat |

## The EQUIPMENT I need

Large bowl
Measuring cup/spoons
Whisk
Cutting board/knife
Grill
Fork or tongs

## &&&&&&&&&&&&&& How To Make It &&&&&&&&&&&&&&&

1. In a large bowl, combine the allspice, thyme, cayenne pepper, black pepper, nutmeg, cinnamon, salt, garlic powder and sugar.
2. With a wire whisk, slowly add the olive oil, soy sauce, vinegar, orange juice and lime juice.
3. Add onion and green onions and mix well.
4. Add the chicken breasts, cover and marinate for at least 1 hour, longer if possible.
5. Preheat grill. Remove the breasts from the marinade and grill for 6 minutes on each side until fully cooked. While grilling baste with the marinade.
6. Heat the leftover marinade and serve on the side for dipping.

Serves 4

# PEANUT PUNCH

## The INGREDIENTS I need

| | |
|---|---|
| 1/2 cup | Peanut Butter |
| 3 cups | Milk |
| 2 Tbsp. | Sugar |
| Pinch | Cinnamon |
| Pinch | Nutmeg |

## The EQUIPMENT I need

Blender
Glass

8888888888888888888 **How To Make It** 8888888888888888

1. Put peanut butter, milk, sugar, cinnamon and nutmeg in blender.
2. Blend on high speed for 25 seconds. It will look thick and frothy.
3. Pour into glasses.

**Serves 2**

# RICE AND PEAS

## The INGREDIENTS I need

| | |
|---|---|
| 1 pound can | Red Kidney Beans or Pigeon Peas |
| 1-1/4 cups | Long Grain Rice |
| 2-1/2 cups | Coconut Milk |
| 2 | Green Onions, chopped |
| 1 small | Onion, chopped |
| 1 clove | Garlic, chopped |
| 1 Tbsp. | Vegetable Oil |
| 1 tsp. | Thyme |
| 1 tsp. | Salt |
| 1/2 tsp. | Pepper |

## The EQUIPMENT I need

Frying pan
Casserole pan
Cutting board/knife
Measuring cup/spoons
Can opener

## ᔕᔕᔕᔕᔕᔕᔕᔕᔕᔕᔕᔕ How To Make It ᔕᔕᔕᔕᔕᔕᔕᔕᔕᔕᔕᔕ

1. Heat the oil in a frying pan.
2. Fry the onions until it is golden brown.
3. Drain the beans and place in a casserole with all the other ingredients.
4. Cover and cook over a very low heat for 20 to 30 minutes until all the liquid is absorbed by the rice.

**Serves 4-6**

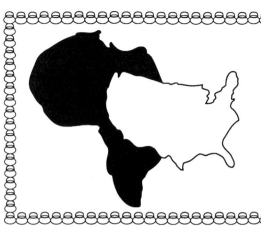

# CREOLE AND CAJUN COOKING

## *Louisiana's Own*

Beignets

Bread Pudding

Crawfish E'Touffée

Creole Gumbo

Creole Jambalaya

Dirty Rice

Gumbo Filé

Okra Gumbo

Red Beans and Rice

Shrimp Creole

# BEIGNETS (French Doughnuts)

## The INGREDIENTS I need

### The EQUIPMENT I need

**Easy Way**

| | | |
|---|---|---|
| 1 can | Refrigerator Biscuits | Measuring cup/spoons |
| | Vegetable Oil | Skillet |
| 1/2 cup | Powdered Sugar | Cutting board/knife |
| 1 | Paper Bag | Tongs |

## ☺☺☺☺☺☺☺☺☺☺☺☺☺☺ How To Make It ☺☺☺☺☺☺☺☺☺☺☺☺☺☺

1. Shape each biscuit into a square.
2. Heat an inch of oil in a skillet until very hot.
3. Drop biscuits into oil.
4. Fry 2 or 3 minutes until brown on both sides.
5. Drain on a paper towel.
6. Put powdered sugar in the paper bag.
7. Put beignets in bag and shake until coated with sugar.

**Serves 4-6**

# BREAD PUDDING

## The INGREDIENTS I need

| | |
|---|---|
| 1 loaf | Stale French Bread |
| 1 quart | Milk |
| 3 | Eggs |
| 3/4 cup | Sugar |
| 1 Tbsp. | Vanilla Extract |
| 1/4 tsp. | Nutmeg |
| 3/4 cup | Raisins |
| 2 Tbsp. | Butter or Margarine, cut into small pieces |

## The EQUIPMENT I need

Bowls
Measuring cup/spoons
Baking Dish, 9-in. x 13-in.
Spoon

## ꙮꙮꙮꙮꙮꙮꙮꙮꙮꙮꙮꙮꙮ How To Make It ꙮꙮꙮꙮꙮꙮꙮꙮꙮꙮꙮꙮꙮ

1. Heat over to 350 degrees.
2. In large bowl place bread torn into pieces.
3. Pour milk over bread; let bread soak.
4. In medium bowl beat eggs, sugar, vanilla extract and nutmeg.
5. Add to milk-soaked bread.
6. Stir to mix well.
7. Add raisins and butter. Stir to mix well.
8. Pour mixture into well-buttered 9-in. x 13-in. baking dish.
9. Bake for 1 hour.

Makes 8 servings

# CRAWFISH E'TOUFÉE

## The INGREDIENTS I need

| | |
|---|---|
| 1/4 cup | Butter or Margarine |
| 2 Tbsp. | Oil |
| 2 Tbsp. | Flour |
| 1/4 cup | Onions, chopped |
| 1/4 cup | Green Pepper, chopped |
| 1/4 cup | Celery, chopped |
| 1/4 cup | Parsley, minced |
| 3 cloves | Garlic, minced |
| 1/4 cup | Green Onions, chopped |
| 2 cups | Water, hot |
| 2 | Bay Leaves |
| 1 tsp. | Salt |
| 1 tsp. | Cayenne Pepper |
| 1 cup | Tomato Sauce |
| 2 pounds | Cooked Crawfish Tails |

## The EQUIPMENT I need

Pot
Cutting board/knife
Measuring cup/spoons
Wooden spoon

## ᪣᪣᪣᪣᪣᪣᪣᪣᪣᪣᪣ How To Make It ᪣᪣᪣᪣᪣᪣᪣᪣᪣᪣᪣

1. In a pot heat butter or margarine and oil.
2. Add flour to hot oil; stir and cook for 5 minutes.
3. Add onions, green peppers, celery and garlic.
4. Slowly add hot water; mix well.
5. Add tomato sauce, green onions, bay leaf, salt and cayenne pepper.
6. Bring to a boil; let simmer for 15 minutes.
7. Add crawfish tails and parsley.
8. Cook about 10 minutes. Serve over rice.

Serves 4

# CREOLE GUMBO

## The INGREDIENTS I need

| | |
|---|---|
| 8 cups | Chicken Broth |
| 1 T. | Thyme |
| 2 | Bay Leaves |
| 3 cloves | Garlic, minced |
| 1/2 tsp. | Garlic Powder |
| 1 large can | Tomatoes |
| 1 tsp. | Oregano |
| 1 tsp. | Onion Powder |
| 1 cup | Celery, chopped |
| 1 1-2 pounds | Shrimp, deveined |
| 1 pt. | Oysters |
| 1 1-2 cups | Crabmeat |
| 2-3 pounds | Chicken, chopped |
| 1 box | Frozen Okra, cut |
| 1 T. | Salt |
| 1/4 tsp. | Caynene Pepper |
| 1/4 tsp. | Black Pepper |

## The EQUIPMENT I need

Pot with lid
Measuring cup/spoons
Knife
Cutting board
Wooden spoon
Can opener

ꝏꝏꝏꝏꝏꝏꝏꝏꝏꝏ How To Make It ꝏꝏꝏꝏꝏꝏꝏꝏꝏꝏ

1. Boil chicken and reserve stock.
2. Add to this, all the ingredients above except the okra and bring to a boil, (about 10 minutes).
3. Simmer for 40 minutes.
4. Add okra, cook for 10 minutes.
5. Serve with rice.

**Serves 6-8**

# CREOLE JAMBALAYA

## The INGREDIENTS I need

| | |
|---|---|
| 1 pound | Smoked Sausage, sliced |
| 1/2 pound | Ham, diced |
| 1 Tbsp. | Oil |
| 2 | Onions, chopped |
| 1 | Green Pepper, chopped |
| 1/2 cup | Celery, chopped |
| 1/2 cup | Green Onions, chopped |
| 1 can | Tomatoes, (16 oz.) |
| 3 cups | Beef, Chicken Stock or Water |
| 2 cloves | Garlic, chopped |
| 1 | Bay Leaf |
| 1/4 tsp. | Pepper |
| 1/2 tsp. | Salt |
| 2 cups | Rice, uncooked |
| 1 pound | Shrimp, peeled and deveined |

## The EQUIPMENT I need

Skillet/Pot
Measuring cup/spoons
Cutting board/knife
Wooden spoon

## ᵃᵃᵃᵃᵃᵃᵃᵃᵃᵃᵃᵃᵃᵃᵃᵃ How To Make It ᵃᵃᵃᵃᵃᵃᵃᵃᵃᵃᵃᵃᵃᵃᵃᵃ

1. Heat oil in skillet.
2. Fry the sausage and ham.
3. Add onion, green pepper, green onions and celery and saute until tender or soft.
4. Add tomatoes, stock or water to pot.
5. Add garlic, bay leaf, pepper, salt and rice.
6. Stir, bring to a boil - then reduce heat.
7. Cover and simmer for 15 minutes.
8. Add water if Jambalaya seems dry.
9. Add shrimp, re-cover and cook 15 minutes longer, mix well.

**Serves 6-8**

# DIRTY RICE (Louisiana Rice Dressing)

## The INGREDIENTS I need

| | |
|---|---|
| 2 cups | Rice |
| 1/2 pound | Chicken Gizzards |
| 1/2 pound | Chicken Livers |
| 1/2 pound | Ground Beef |
| 1 cup | Onions, chopped |
| 1 | Green Pepper, chopped |
| 1/2 cup | Celery, chopped |
| 2 cloves | Garlic, chopped |
| 1 Tbsp. | Parsley, chopped |
| 2 | Green Onions, chopped |
| Dash | Salt |
| Dash | Pepper |

## The EQUIPMENT I need

Pot
Cutting board/knife
Measuring cup/spoons
Skillet
Casserole/Baking dish
Wooden spoon

## ᎧᎧᎧᎧᎧᎧᎧᎧᎧᎧᎧᎧᎧᎧ How To Make It ᎧᎧᎧᎧᎧᎧᎧᎧᎧᎧᎧᎧᎧᎧ

1. Place gizzards and livers in pot and add water to cover.
2. Boil for 10 minutes.
3. Add ground beef to skillet and mix well.
4. Pour off oil and drain.
5. Add chopped onions, garlic, celery, green peppers, green onions and parsley.
6. Cook over medium heat 15 minutes.
7. Remove livers and gizzards from water and chop well.
8. Add to mixture; stir well.
9. Stir rice into mixture with salt and pepper.
10. Pour into casserole dish or baking dish and heat in oven at 350 degrees for 15 minutes.

**Serves 6-8**

# GUMBO FILÉ

## The INGREDIENTS I need

| | |
|---|---|
| 2 sticks | Margarine |
| 1 cup | Celery, chopped |
| 1 cup | Onion, chopped |
| 1 Tbsp. | Fresh or Dried Parsley, chopped |
| 1/2 cup | Green Pepper, chopped |
| 2 Tbsp. | Garlic, minced |
| 16 cups | Water |
| 1/2 cup | Flour |
| 2 | Bay Leaves |
| 1 pound | Hot Links, (Sausage) |
| 6 | Crabs |
| 1/2 pound | Smoked Ham, diced |
| 1/2 pound | Shrimp, Peeled and deveined |
| 1 Tbsp. | Thyme |
| 1/4 tsp. | Salt |
| 1/4 tsp. | Pepper |
| 2 Tbsp. | Filé Powder |

## The EQUIPMENT I need

Large pot-lid
Measuring cup/spoons
Wooden spoon
Cutting board/knife

## How To Make It

1. Place margarine in large pot.
2. Add celery, onion, parsley, green pepper and garlic.
3. Sauté and then simmer for 15 minutes over low heat.
4. Add flour and stir constantly for 15 minutes.
5. Add water and bay leaves.
6. Heat for 20 minutes, stir in ham, crab and sausages and cook for 30 minutes.
7. Bring to boil; add shrimp, thyme, salt and pepper.
8. Stir in filé powder; serve over rice.

Serves 8-10

# OKRA GUMBO

## The INGREDIENTS I need

| | |
|---|---|
| 2 pounds | Shrimp |
| 16 cups | Chicken Stock (1 gallon) |
| 1/3 cup | Butter |
| 2 pounds | Okra, sliced |
| 1 large | Onion, chopped |
| 1 | Green Pepper, chopped |
| 1 clove | Garlic, minced |
| 2 Tbsp. | Parsley, chopped |
| 1-1/2 cups | Canned Tomatoes (#2 can) |

## The EQUIPMENT I need

Measuring cups
Wooden spoon
Soup pot
Cutting board/knife
Can opener

## පපපපපපපපපපපපපපප How To Make It පපපපපපපපපපපපපපප

1. Peel and clean shrimp.
2. Melt butter in soup pot.
3. Add okra, onion, green pepper and saute.
4. Add garlic and chopped parsley and cook for 2 minutes.
5. Add chicken stock and tomatoes.
6. Add shrimp and cook over medium heat for 30 minutes.
7. Stir thoroughly. Serve with rice.

**Makes 8 servings**

# RED BEANS AND RICE

## The INGREDIENTS I need

## The EQUIPMENT I need

| | | |
|---|---|---|
| 2 cups | Red (Kidney Beans) | Pot |
| 6 cups | Water, cold | Measuring cup/spoons |
| 1 large | Onion, chopped | Cutting board/knife |
| 1 | Green Pepper, chopped | Wooden spoon |
| 1/2 pound | Ham (cubed) or | |
| 1/2 pound | Smoked Sausage (sliced) | |
| 2 cloves | Garlic, chopped | |
| 1 | Bay Leaf | |
| 1/2 tsp. | Salt | |
| 1/2 tsp. | Pepper | |

## ᵒᵒᵒᵒᵒᵒᵒᵒᵒᵒᵒᵒᵒᵒᵒᵒ How To Make It ᵒᵒᵒᵒᵒᵒᵒᵒᵒᵒᵒᵒᵒᵒᵒᵒ

1. Wash beans in cold water.
2. Drain beans and put in covered pot with cold water.
3. Add ham or sausage to pot, bring to boil slowly.
4. Add chopped onion,s, garlic, green pepper, bay leaf,
   salt and pepper.
5. Simmer for 2 hours stirring occasionally until beans are soft.
6. Mash some of the beans against the side of the pot to make
   a creamy sauce.
7. Serve with rice.

6 servings

# SHRIMP CREOLE

## The INGREDIENTS I need

| | |
|---|---|
| 1 cup | Celery, chopped |
| 4 | Green Onions, chopped |
| 1/2 cup | Green Pepper, chopped |
| 1/4 cup | Butter |
| 2 Tbsp. | Flour |
| 1 tsp. | Salt |
| 1/2 tsp. | Pepper |
| 1 tsp. | Garlic, minced |
| 1 can | Tomato Paste |
| 1 cup | Water |
| 2 pounds | Shrimp, deveined and shelled |

## The EQUIPMENT I need

Skillet
Measuring cup/spoons
Wooden spoon
Cutting board/knife

## ᴆᴆᴆᴆᴆᴆᴆᴆᴆᴆᴆᴆᴆᴆᴆ How To Make It ᴆᴆᴆᴆᴆᴆᴆᴆᴆᴆᴆᴆᴆᴆᴆ

1. Cook celery, onion and green pepper in butter.
2. Blend in flour and seasonings.
3. Stir in tomato paste and water.
4. Cover and simmer for 30 minutes.
5. Add shrimps; simmer for 10 minutes.
6. Serve over cooked rice.

**Serves 6**

# AFRICAN-AMERICAN HERITAGE

# HOLIDAY DISHES

## January

**New Year's Day 1**
Chitlin Pig's Feet
Baked Fish Fish
Hoppin' John
Collard Greens and Ham Hocks
Crackling Cornbread
Sweet Potato Pie

**Dr. Martin Luther King Jr. Birthday 15th**
Smothered Chicken
Rice
Mixed Greens with Turnips
Buttermilk Poundcake

## February

**Black History Month**
Fried Chicken
Black-eyed Peas
Smothered Cabbage
Okra & Corn & Tomato
Cornbread
Fried Pies

**Mardi Gras**
Creole Gumbo
Jambalaya
Red Beans & Rice
Bread Pudding
Pecan Pie

## March/April

**Easter**
Ham
Lamb
Macaroni and Cheese
Peas and Carrots
Potato Salad
Rolls
Coconut Cake

## June

**Juneteenth 19**
Barbecued Ribs and Chicken
Hot Links
Steaks
Potato Salad
Baked Beans
Turnip and Mustard Greens
Garlic Bread
Watermelon
Peach Cobbler
Strawberry Soda

## July

**Independence Day 4th**
Barbecued Chicken Ribs Beef
Hamburger
Hot Dogs
Macaroni Salad
Baked Beans
Deviled Eggs
Corn-on-the-Cob
Pineapple Upside-Down Cake
Corn Muffins
Lemonade

## August

**Family Reunions**
Fried Chicken
Fried Crabcakes
Chili Beans
Hamburger Hot Dogs
Coleslaw
Fried Corn
Hoecakes
Fresh Fruit
Peach Cobbler
Tea Cakes
Iced Tea

## November

**Thanksgiving**
Roast Turkey
Ham
Cornbread Dressing
Giblet Gravy
String Beans
Sweet Potato Pudding
with Marshmellows
Cranberry Mold
Ambrosia
Refrigerator Rolls
Sweet Potato Pie
Pound Cake

## December

**Christmas 25**
Roast Turkey Roast Beef
Herb Stuffing Gravy
Candied Yams Greens
Monkey Bread Egg Nog
Holiday Fruitcake

**Kwanzaa Dec.26-Jan.1**
Baked Fish
Chicken in Groundnut Sauce
Jollof Rice
Candied Yam or Dun Dun
African Salad
Fried Plantains
African Slush Punch

## Traditional

**Sunday Dinner**
Southern Fried Chicken
Pineapple Glazed Ham
Green Beans with Potatoes
Old-Fashioned Potato Salad
Tomato and Onions
Vinaigrette
Lemon Meringue Pie
Pound Cake
Dinner Rolls

## Friday Night

**Fish Fry**
Fried Fish
French Fried Sweet Potatoes
Coleslaw
Hush Puppies
Apple Brown Betty

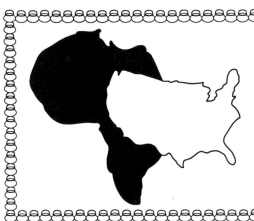

# GEORGE WASHINGTON CARVER'S
## *Peanut Recipes*

African Peanut Butter Chicken

Boiled Peanuts

Homemade Peanut Butter

Peanut Butter Biscuits

Peanut Butter Bread

Peanut Brittle

Peanut Butter Cookies

Peanut Butter Muffins

Peanut Butter Pancakes

Peanut Butter Soup

Peanut Pie

Grond Nut Stew

# GEORGE WASHINGTON CARVER
# (1864-1943)

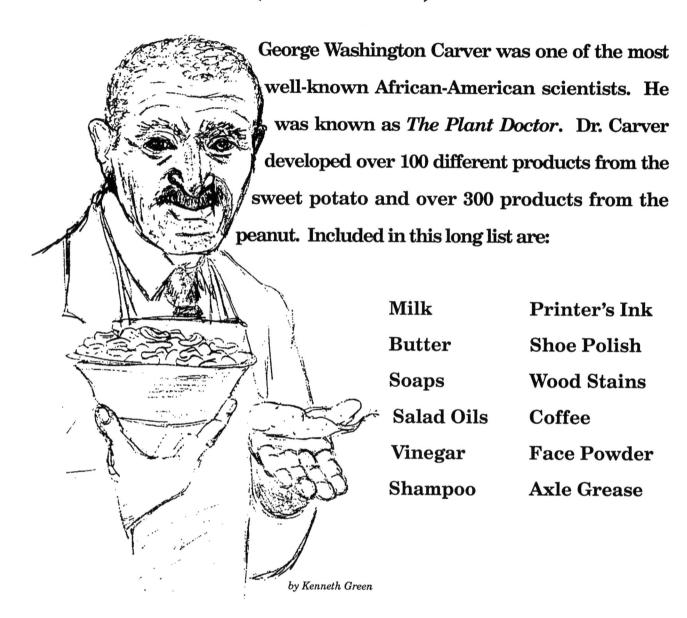

George Washington Carver was one of the most well-known African-American scientists. He was known as *The Plant Doctor*. Dr. Carver developed over 100 different products from the sweet potato and over 300 products from the peanut. Included in this long list are:

| | |
|---|---|
| Milk | Printer's Ink |
| Butter | Shoe Polish |
| Soaps | Wood Stains |
| Salad Oils | Coffee |
| Vinegar | Face Powder |
| Shampoo | Axle Grease |

*by Kenneth Green*

Dr. Carver published 100 cooking recipes using the peanut as a base. He wrote *How to Grow the Peanut and 105 Ways of Preparing It For Human Consumption*. Dr. Carver taught at Tuskegee Institute in Alabama from 1896 to 1943.

# AFRICAN PEANUT BUTTER CHICKEN

## The INGREDIENTS I need

| | |
|---|---|
| 2 pounds | Chicken, cut up |
| 1 large | Onion, chopped |
| 1 | Green Pepper, chopped |
| 1 cup | Flour |
| 1 clove | Garlic , minced |
| 1/4 cup | Peanut Oil |
| 1 cup | Water |
| 1/2 | Red Pepper, chopped |
| 1/4 tsp. | Cayenne Pepper |
| 1/4 tsp. | Black Pepper |
| 1/8 tsp. | Salt |
| 1 cup | Peanut Butter |
| 1/2 cup | Peanuts, chopped |

## The EQUIPMENT I need

Skillet
Measuring cup/spoons
Wooden spoon
Cutting board/knife
Fork

## ❸❸❸❸❸❸❸❸❸❸❸❸❸ How To Make It ❸❸❸❸❸❸❸❸❸❸❸❸❸

1. Cut chicken into pieces, flour and fry in skillet with oil; remove when brown.
2. Saute onion, peppers and garlic in pan for 5 minutes.
3. Add chicken, water and dry ingredients and simmer over low heat 30 minutes.
4. Add peanut butter and peanuts; let simmer 30 minutes.
5. Serve over rice.

Serves 6-8

# BOILED PEANUTS

## The INGREDIENTS I need

|  |  |
|---|---|
|  | Green Peanuts in Shell |
| 2 Tbsp. | Salt |

## The EQUIPMENT I need

Pot
Measuring Spoon

∽∽∽∽∽∽∽∽∽∽∽∽∽∽∽∽ **How To Make It** ∽∽∽∽∽∽∽∽∽∽∽∽∽∽∽∽

1. In cool water, rinse peanuts in shell.
2. Place in large saucepan with water to cover.
3. Add salt to pot.
4. Cover and bring to boil, reduce heat to low simmer.
5. Cook for 45 minutes until shells are tender. Drain.
6. When cool, shell and eat.

# HOMEMADE PEANUT BUTTER

## The INGREDIENTS I need

| | |
|---|---|
| 2 cups | Raw Peanuts, shelled and skinned |
| 1 to 1-1/2 Tbsp. | Peanut Oil Oil |
| 1/2 tsp. | Salt (optional) |

## The EQUIPMENT I need

Baking pan
Food processor with metal blade
Spatula
Jar/container with lid
Measuring cup/spoons

## ᘉᘉᘉᘉᘉᘉᘉᘉᘉᘉᘉᘉᘉᘉᘉᘉᘉ How To Make It ᘉᘉᘉᘉᘉᘉᘉᘉᘉᘉᘉᘉᘉᘉᘉᘉᘉ

1. Preheat over to 350 degrees.
2. In large shallow baking pan roast shelled nuts 15-20 minutes or nuts in shell 25 minutes.
3. Remove from oven and cool.
4. Put the peanuts, oil and salt in a food processor with metal blade.
5. Pulse the machine to chop the nuts coarsely, until peanut butter has a smooth creamy consistency—2-3 minutes.
6. Scrap into jar or container with an airtight lid; store in refrigerator.
7. If oil rises to the top of the container, stir it back in or pour it off before using peanut butter.

Makes 1 cup

# PEANUT BUTTER BISCUITS

## The INGREDIENTS I need

| | |
|---|---|
| 2 cups | Sifted Flour, white or wheat |
| 4 tsp. | Baking Powder |
| 1/2 tsp. | Salt |
| 2 Tbsp. | Butter or Margarine |
| 1/4 cup | Peanut Butter |
| 1/2 cup | Milk |

## The EQUIPMENT I need

Bowl
Sifter
Measuring cup/spoons
Wooden spoon
Rolling pin
Baking sheet

## 8888888888888888 How To Make It 8888888888888888

1. Combine flour, baking powder and salt and sift together into a bowl.
2. Stir in the peanut butter and butter.
3. Add milk to make a dough that is soft but easy to handle.
4. Knead very gently for a minute.
5. Roll out to a 1/2 inch thickness and cut into rounds with a biscuit cutter.
6. Place on greased baking sheet.
7. Bake at 450 degrees about 15 minutes.

Makes 12

# PEANUT BUTTER BREAD

## The INGREDIENTS I need

2 cups    Flour
4 tsp.    Baking Powder
1 tsp.    Salt
1/2 cup    Sugar
1 cup    Milk
2/3 cup    Peanut Butter
           Vegetable Oil Spray

## The EQUIPMENT I need

Loaf pan
Sifter
Measuring cup/spoons
Bowl
Wooden spoon

## 8888888888888888 How To Make It 8888888888888888

1. Sift flour, baking powder and salt.
2. Add peanut butter and sugar.
3. Add milk, mix thoroughly.
4. Pour into well greased baking pan.
5. Bake at 450 degrees about 30 minutes.

Makes 1 medium loaf

# PEANUT BRITTLE

## The INGREDIENTS I need

2 cups      Sugar
1 cup       Light Corn Syrup
2 cups      Raw Peanuts
2 tsp.      Baking Soda
2 Tbsp.     Butter or Margarine
1 tsp.      Salt

## The EQUIPMENT I need

Saucepan
Measuring cup/spoons
Wooden spoon
Cookie sheet

## ∞∞∞∞∞∞∞∞∞∞∞∞∞ How To Make It ∞∞∞∞∞∞∞∞∞∞∞∞∞

1. Cook sugar and corn syrup together until sugar is dissolved.
2. Add peanuts and cook until mixture turns a gold brown color.
3. Add butter, salt and baking soda.
4. Stir and pour onto buttered cookie sheet, spreading quickly to cover surfaces.
5. Break into pieces when cool.

**Serves 4-5**

# PEANUT BUTTER COOKIES

## The INGREDIENTS I need

| | |
|---|---|
| 1/2 cup | Margarine |
| 1/2 cup | Chunky Peanut Butter |
| 1/2 cup | Brown Sugar, light |
| 1/2 cup | Sugar |
| 1/2 tsp. | Vanilla |
| 1 | Egg |
| 1-1/2 cup | Flour |
| 1 tsp. | Baking Soda |
| 1 tsp. | Salt |

## The EQUIPMENT I need

Cookie sheet
Measuring cup/spoons
Bowl
Sifter
Wooden spoon

## 8888888888888888 How To Make It 8888888888888888

1. Cream margarine with peanut butter.
2. Add sugars and vanilla gradually, creaming until fluffy.
3. Fold in egg.
4. Sift flour, soda and salt together and stir into mixture.
5. Shape into 1-inch balls and place 2 inches apart on an ungreased cookie sheet.
6. Flatten with fork.
7. Bake at 375 degrees for 10-12 minutes.

Makes 48 cookies

# PEANUT BUTTER MUFFINS

## The INGREDIENTS I need

| | |
|---|---|
| 1 cup | Flour, white or wheat |
| 1 Tbsp. | Baking Powder |
| 1/2 tsp. | Salt |
| 1/2 cup | Peanut Butter |
| 2 Tbsp. | Honey |
| 1 | Egg, beaten |
| 2/3 cup | Milk |

## The EQUIPMENT I need

Muffin pan
Bowl
Measuring cup/spoons
Wooden spoon

## ᘗᘗᘗᘗᘗᘗᘗᘗᘗᘗᘗᘗᘗᘗᘗᘗ How To Make It ᘗᘗᘗᘗᘗᘗᘗᘗᘗᘗᘗᘗᘗᘗᘗᘗ

1. In bowl, blend together all the dry ingredients.
2. In another bowl, blend together the remaining ingredients.
3. Pour into the dry ingredients. Blend well.
4. Pour into muffin pans.
5. Bake at 425 degrees for 15 minutes.

**Makes 12**

# PEANUT BUTTER PANCAKES

## The INGREDIENTS I need

| | |
|---|---|
| 2 cups | Milk |
| 1/2 cup | Peanut Butter |
| 2 | Eggs |
| 1 Tbsp. | Peanut Oil |
| 2 cups | Pancake Mix |

## The EQUIPMENT I need

Griddle/skillet
Measuring cup/spoons
Bowl
Wooden spoon
Spatula

## ᎧᎧᎧᎧᎧᎧᎧᎧᎧᎧᎧ How To Make It ᎧᎧᎧᎧᎧᎧᎧᎧᎧᎧᎧ

1. Combine milk, peanut butter, eggs and oil in a mixing bowl.
2. Beat until well blended.
3. Add pancake mix, stir lightly until batter is smooth.
4. For each pancake pour about 1/4 cup of batter on a hot, lightly oiled griddle or skillet.
5. Turn when bubbles appear on surface.

Serves 4-6

# PEANUT BUTTER SOUP

## The INGREDIENTS I need

| | |
|---|---|
| 1/2 cup | Onions, chopped fine |
| 2 Tbsp. | Butter or Margarine |
| 1/2 cup | Peanut Butter |
| 1 10-3/4 oz. | Condensed Cream of Chicken Soup, (can) |
| 2-1/2 cups | Milk |
| 1/4 tsp. | Cayenne Pepper |

## The EQUIPMENT I need

Saucepan
Cutting board/knife
Measuring cup/spoons
Wooden spoon

## ❀❀❀❀❀❀❀❀❀❀❀❀❀❀❀❀ How To Make It ❀❀❀❀❀❀❀❀❀❀❀❀❀❀❀❀

1. In saucepan sauté onion in butter or margarine, stirring constantly until onions are light brown—about 5 minutes.
2. Add peanut butter and cook 3 minutes, stirring constantly.
3. Stir in soup, milk and pepper.
4. Heat thoroughly but do not boil.

**Serves 4-6**

# PEANUT PIE

## The INGREDIENTS I need

| | |
|---|---|
| 1 cup | Dark Corn Syrup |
| 4 | Eggs, well beaten |
| 1/2 cup | White Sugar |
| 2 Tbsp. | Butter or Margarine melted |
| 3 Tbsp. | Flour, sifted |
| 1/4 tsp. | Salt |
| 1 cup | Roasted Peanuts |
| 1 | Pie Shell, unbaked, frozen |

## The EQUIPMENT I need

Measuring cup/spoons
Bowl
Sifter
Wooden spoon

## ଆଆଆଆଆଆଆଆଆଆଆଆଆଆଆ How To Make It ଆଆଆଆଆଆଆଆଆଆଆଆଆଆଆ

1. Beat the eggs; add corn syrup, sugar, butter or margarine, flour and salt.
2. Blend thoroughly. Fold in the nuts.
3. Pour into unbaked pie shell.
4. Bake at 350 degrees 30 to 40 minutes.

Serves 6-8

# GROUND NUT STEW

## The INGREDIENTS I need

| | |
|---|---|
| 2 cups | Water |
| 1 | Chicken, cut into pieces |
| 2 Tbsp. | Tomato Paste |
| 1 Tbsp. | Peanut Oil |
| 1 cup | Onion, chopped |
| 1 cup | Tomatoes, chopped or |
| 14-1/2 oz. | Can of Diced Tomatoes |
| 2/3 cup | Peanut Butter |
| 1 tsp. | Salt |
| 1 tsp. | Cayenne Pepper |
| 1/2 tsp. | Curry Powder |
| 1/2 tsp. | Dried Thyme |
| 2 cloves | Garlic, chopped |
| 1 medium | Eggplant, peeled and cubed |
| 2 cups | Okra, fresh or frozen |

## The EQUIPMENT I need

2 pots
Measuring cup/spoons
Wooden spoon
Cutting board/knife

## ঃঃঃঃঃঃঃঃঃঃঃঃঃঃঃ How To Make It ঃঃঃঃঃঃঃঃঃঃঃঃঃঃঃ

1. Boil chicken in water.
2. In large pot, fry tomato paste in the oil over low heat for five minutes.
3. Add to the paste, onions and tomatoes; stir.
4. Remove the cooked chicken pieces and put them, along with half the broth in the large pot.
5. Add the peanut butter and seasoning.
6. Cook for 5 minute before stirring in the eggplants and okra.
7. Cook until chicken and vegetables are tender.
8. Add more broth as needed to maintain a thick, stewy consistency.

Serves 4-6

# GEORGE WASHINGTON CARVER'S
## *Sweet Potato Recipes*

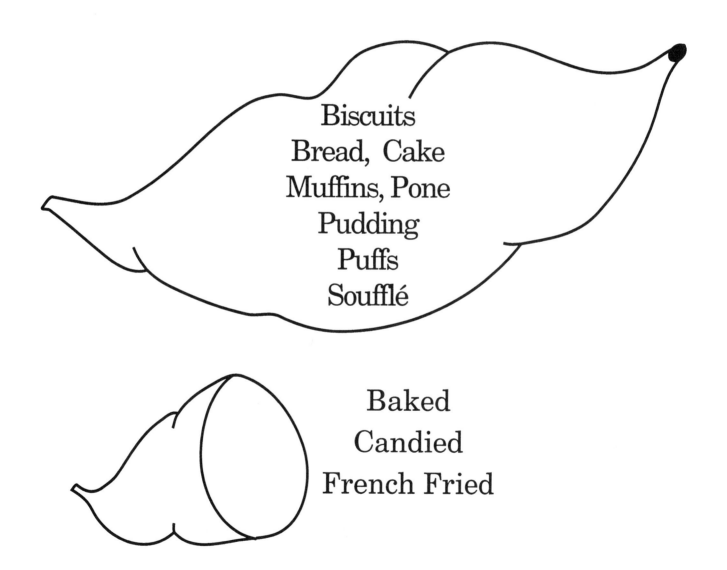

Biscuits
Bread, Cake
Muffins, Pone
Pudding
Puffs
Soufflé

Baked

Candied

French Fried

# BAKED SWEET POTATOES

## The INGREDIENTS I need

| | |
|---|---|
| 2 | Sweet Potatoes |
| 1 Tbsp. | Vegetable Oil |
| 2 Tbsp. | Butter or Margarine |

## The EQUIPMENT I need

Measuring spoon
Fork
Cookie sheet

88888888888888888 **How To Make It** 88888888888888888

1. Preheat over to 350 degrees.
2. Wash sweet potatoes and dry well.
3. Grease the outside of the potatoes with oil.
4. Prick the skins with a fork.
5. Place on cookie sheet.
6. Bake at 350 degrees for 50 minutes.
7. Split open each potato and add butter.

**MICROWAVE**

1. Pierce skin of 2 sweet potatoes.
2. Lay on paper towel for 5-6 minutes.
3. Add butter to potatoes.

**Serves 2**

# CANDIED SWEET POTATOES

## The INGREDIENTS I need

| | |
|---|---|
| 2 large | Yams or Sweet Potatoes, fresh or canned |
| 4 Tbsp. | Butter or Margarine |
| 1/2 cup | Sugar |
| 1/2 cup | Brown Sugar |
| 1/2 cup | Water |
| 1/4 tsp. | Salt |
| 1/2 tsp. | Nutmeg |
| 1 tsp. | Cinnamon |

## The EQUIPMENT I need

Casserole pan
Measuring cup/spoons
Cutting board/knife

## ∞∞∞∞∞∞∞∞∞∞∞∞∞ How To Make It ∞∞∞∞∞∞∞∞∞∞∞∞∞

1. Preheat over to 425 degrees.
2. Peel and cut potatoes in 1/4 to 1/2 inch slices.
3. Place potatoes in casserole pan. Cut butter or margarine into small pieces. Dot potatoes with butter or margarine.
4. Sprinkle the remaining ingredients over the potatoes.
5. Bake uncovered in the oven for one hour.

Serves 4

# FRENCH FRIED SWEET POTATOES

## The INGREDIENTS I need

4 medium  Sweet Potatoes
          Vegetable Oil
          Sugar
          Salt or Cinnamon

## The EQUIPMENT I need

Vegetable peeler
Cutting board/knife
Skillet
Tongs

ꝸꝸꝸꝸꝸꝸꝸꝸꝸꝸꝸꝸꝸꝸ **How To Make It** ꝸꝸꝸꝸꝸꝸꝸꝸꝸꝸꝸꝸꝸ

1. Peel and slice raw sweet potatoes in 1/2 inch slices.
2. Heat vegetable or peanut oil in a heavy skillet.
3. Drop slices a few at a time into hot oil and fry
   until browned—about 5 minutes.
4. Drain on paper towel.
5. Sprinkle them with salt, sugar or cinnamon.

**Serves 2**

# SWEET POTATO BISCUITS

## The INGREDIENTS I need

| | |
|---|---|
| 2 cups | Flour |
| 3 tsp. | Baking Powder |
| 1 tsp. | Salt |
| 1/2 tsp. | Baking Soda |
| 2 Tbsp. | Brown Sugar |
| 1/2 cup | Butter or Margarine, melted |
| 3/4 cup | Buttermilk |
| 1 cup | Sweet Potatoes or Yam, mashed |
| Dash | Cinnamon |

## The EQUIPMENT I need

Small pot
Baking or cookie sheet
Measuring cup/spoons
Mixing bowl
Sifter
Wooden spoon
Electric mixer
Rolling pin
Biscuit cutter

## ꕛꕛꕛꕛꕛꕛꕛꕛꕛꕛꕛꕛꕛꕛ How To Make It ꕛꕛꕛꕛꕛꕛꕛꕛꕛꕛꕛꕛꕛꕛ

1. Combine sifted flour, baking powder and salt and sift together into a mixing bowl.
2. Combine mashed potatoes with brown sugar and margarine or butter. Beat until well blended and fluffy.
3. Dissolve baking soda in buttermilk.
4. Alternately add buttermilk and potato mixture to dry ingredients, stirring only until moist but mixing as little as possible.
5. Turn out onto floured surface and roll out 1/2 inch thick.
6. Cut with biscuit cutter.
7. Place on ungreased baking sheet.
8. Bake at 425 degrees for 15 minutes.

**Makes 15 biscuits**

# SWEET POTATO BREAD

## The INGREDIENTS I need

3 medium Sweet Potatoes or Yams
    (2 large will do as well)
1/2 cup   Butter or Margarine
2 Tbsp.   Sugar
1/2 tsp.   Nutmeg
1/2 tsp.   Cinnamon
1/2 tsp.   Allspice
1/4 tsp.   Salt
5 Tbsp.   Flour
2         Eggs, beaten

## The EQUIPMENT I need

Pot
Electric mixer
Mixing bowl
Measuring cup/spoons
Wooden spoon
Baking pan (8"x 8")

## How To Make It

1. Preheat over to 425 degrees.
2. Boil the potatoes and mash thoroughly.
3. Stir in the butter or margarine until it melts.
4. Add the sugar, spices, salt and flour to the cooled potatoes and beat well.
5. Stir in the beaten eggs and pour the batter into a well-greased baking pan.
6. Bake at 425 degrees for 30 minutes.

**Serves 6**

# SWEET POTATO CAKE

## The INGREDIENTS I need

| | |
|---|---|
| 1-1/2 cups | Sifted Flour |
| 2 tsp. | Baking Powder |
| 1/4 tsp. | Salt |
| 2 cups | Sweet Potatoes, hot, boiled and mashed |
| 1/2 cup | Shortening |
| 2 | Eggs, well beaten |
| 3/4 cup | Brown Sugar |
| 1/2 tsp. | Cinnamon |
| 1/2 tsp. | Nutmeg |
| 1/2 cup | Milk |
| 1 Tbsp. | Lemon Juice |

## The EQUIPMENT I need

Bowl
Measuring cup/spoons
Sifter
Wooden spoon
Electric mixer
Loaf pan

## &&&&&&&&&&&&&&& How To Make It &&&&&&&&&&&&&&&

1. Combine flour, baking powder and salt and sift into mixing bowl.
2. To the mashed potatoes, add shortening, eggs, brown sugar, cinnamon and nutmeg. Beat well.
3. Alternately add the flour mixture and milk, beating well after each addition.
4. Add lemon juice and turn into greased loaf pan.
5. Bake at 350 degrees for 1 hour or until done.

Serves 4-6

# SWEET POTATO MUFFINS

## The INGREDIENTS I need

1 pound  Sweet Potatoes
2 Tbsp.  Butter or Margarine
         (room temperature)
1/4 tsp.  Salt
2 Tbsp.  Sugar
1/2 cup  Milk
2        Eggs, beaten
1 cup    Flour
2 tsp.   Baking Powder
Pinch    Baking Soda
         Vegetable Oil Spray

## The EQUIPMENT I need

Pot
Muffin pan
Measuring cup/spoons
Mixing bowl
Fork
Wooden spoon

## ᵃᵃᵃᵃᵃᵃᵃᵃᵃᵃᵃᵃᵃᵃᵃᵃ How To Make It ᵃᵃᵃᵃᵃᵃᵃᵃᵃᵃᵃᵃᵃᵃᵃᵃ

1. Preheat oven to 375 degrees.
2. Boil potatoes in water to cover until tender.
3. Drain and peel off skin.
4. Place in mixing bowl and mash until smooth.
5. Beat in butter, salt and sugar.
6. Combine milk and eggs.  Add flour to form a soft dough.
7. Add baking powder and soda and mix well.
8. Teaspoon into greased muffin pan.
9. Bake for 15 minutes.

Makes 24 muffins

# SWEET POTATO PONE

## The INGREDIENTS I need

| | |
|---|---|
| 4 cups | Sweet Potatoes, grated raw |
| 2 cups | Dark Molasses |
| 1 cup | Brown Sugar |
| 1 tsp. | Cinnamon |
| 1/4 cup | Seedless Raisins |
| 1 cup | Warm Water |
| 2 Tbsp. | Orange Rind, grated |
| 1 Tbsp. | Lemon Rind, grated |
| 1/2 tsp. | Ginger |
| 2 Tbsp. | Coconut, grated |
| | Vegetable Oil Spray |

## The EQUIPMENT I need

Baking pan
Bowl
Measuring cup/spoons
Wooden spoon
Grater

## How To Make It

1. Preheat oven to 325 degrees.
2. In large bowl combine all the ingredients.
3. Beat mixture well to blend.
4. Grease baking pan with vegetable oil spray.
5. Pour into pan.
6. Bake for 1 hour or until crust forms on top.

Makes 8

# SWEET POTATO PUDDING

## The INGREDIENTS I need

| | |
|---|---|
| 1 cup | Sweet Potato, mashed, cooked |
| 2 Tbsp. | Butter or Margarine, melted |
| 1/3 cup | Dark Brown Sugar |
| 1/3 cup | White Sugar |
| 2 | Eggs, well beaten |
| 1 tsp. | Vanilla |
| 1/3 cup | Orange Juice |

## The EQUIPMENT I need

Measuring cup/spoons
Quart casserole
Bowl
Wooden spoon

88888888888888888 **How To Make It** 88888888888888888

1. Preheat oven to 350 degrees. Grease casserole.
2. Mix the ingredient well.
3. Pour into casserole.
4. Bake uncovered for 30 minutes.
5. Serve hot or cold.

**Serves 4**

# SWEET POTATO PUFFS

## The INGREDIENTS I need

| | |
|---|---|
| 2 | Eggs, beaten |
| 2 cups | Sweet Potatoes or Canned Yams, mashed |
| 1 cup | Flour |
| 1-1/2 tsp. | Baking Powder |
| 1/2 tsp. | Salt |
| 1/4 tsp. | Cinnamon |
| 1/4 tsp. | Nutmeg |

## The EQUIPMENT I need

Pot
Skillet
Measuring cup/spoons
Sifter
Rolling pin
Biscuit cutter
Tongs
Paper towel

## ∞∞∞∞∞∞∞∞∞∞∞∞∞ How To Make It ∞∞∞∞∞∞∞∞∞∞∞∞∞

1. Cook sweet potatoes until tender.
2. Drain and mash.
3. Sift in dry ingredients together.
4. Beat eggs and potatoes together and add dry ingredients.
5. Roll out 1/2 inch thick. Cut out circles with biscuit cutter.
6. Fry in oil for 2-3 minutes.
7. Drain on paper towel.
8. Sprinkle with sugar.

Serves 4-6

# SWEET POTATO SOUFFLÉ

## The INGREDIENTS I need

| | |
|---|---|
| 4 cups | Yams, fresh or canned, hot boiled |
| 4 Tbsp. | Butter or Margarine |
| 1/4 cup | Honey |
| 1 | Egg Yolk |
| 1 cup | Orange Juice or Milk |
| 2 Tbsp. | Brown Sugar |
| 1/2 tsp. | Mace |
| 1/4 tsp. | Nutmeg |
| 1 tsp. | Salt |
| 2 | Egg Whites |

## The EQUIPMENT I need

Pot
Casserole pan
Measuring cup/spoons
Wooden spoon
Electric mixer

ꙮꙮꙮꙮꙮꙮꙮꙮꙮꙮꙮꙮꙮꙮ **How To Make It** ꙮꙮꙮꙮꙮꙮꙮꙮꙮꙮꙮꙮꙮꙮ

1. Mash the cooked yams while hot.
2. Stir in the butter or margarine, honey and beaten egg yolks.
3. Beat the mixture until fluffy.
4. Mix the orange juice or milk with the brown sugar, mace, nutmeg and salt.
5. Add it slowly to the yam mixture, beating constantly.
6. Beat the egg whites until very stiff and fold them gently into the yam mixture.
7. Pour into buttered casserole and bake in a preheated oven at 300 degrees for 30-35 minutes or until light brown and well puffed.

**Serves 6-8**

## ROOTS FROM YOUR KITCHEN

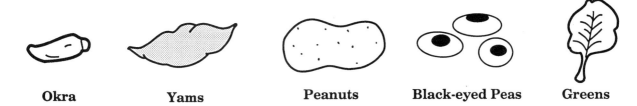

Okra  Yams  Peanuts  Black-eyed Peas  Greens

### ASHCAKES
Cornbread that has been baked in the ashes of open fire.

### BARBECUE
A method of cooking food on a grill over charcoal or open fire. Very popular at social gatherings for African American families during 4th of July, family reunions, picnics and Juneteenth old fashioned cookouts.

### BEIGNETS
Called French doughnuts, they are yeast doughnuts cut into rectangles, deep fried and served hot with powdered sugar. Very popular in New Orleans.

### BISCUIT
The classic quick breakfast bread served throughout the South. They are usually round in shape and light and fluffy in texture. The different types of biscuits are buttermilk, baking powder and ham biscuts.

### BLACK-EYED PEAS
Small tan peas with a black eye. These peas were brought to the southern states from Africa in the 17th century with the slave trade. These peas are a favorite in African-American cooking. They are served either fresh or dried and are eaten in Hoppin' John on New Years Day.

### BRUNSWICK STEW
A southern American stew originally made with squirrel or whatever game was available, but now mostly made with chicken and a variety of vegetables.

### CALLALOO
A leafy vegetable very similar to spinach in flavor and apearance. It is the main ingredient in soup that bears its name and is seasoned with crab. Used in Caribbean and West African cooking.

### CASSAVA
A white root vegetable, shaped like a sweet potato, and containing a large amount of starch. Used in West African and Caribbean cooking.

## CATFISH
A fresh and saltwater fish with slick, scaleless skin, sharp poisonous spine and whiskers. It is very popular in the southern states—usually deep fried in cornmeal.

## CHITTERLINGS OR CHITLINGS
The small intestines of pigs. Popular in African-American cooking during Christmas and New Year.

## COBBLER
A deep-dish fruit pie with a thick top crust and sometimes a bottom crust, usually made with peaches or blueberries.

## COUSCOUS
A special type of wheat (semolina) grown in North Africa. It is a fine, small-grained wheat, served over meat and vegetables.

## COLLARD GREENS
Came to America from Africa and are very popular in the South. Fresh collards are best in the winter after they've been through the first frost of the season. They have a mild cabbage flavor and also come frozen.

## CORN BREAD
A crisp and crunchy bread made from coarsely ground corn. Very popular in African-American cooking. Cornbread is traditionally eaten with greens.

## CORNMEAL
Coarsely ground dried corn, yellow or white. Very popular in African-American cooking for frying fish, making breads such as cornbread, hot water cornbread and hush puppies.

## CORN PONE
Cornmeal dough, shaped into ovals and deep-fried or baked—a southern American bread served with butter and sometimes pot liquor.

## COW PEAS
Also called Black-eyed Peas.

## CRACKLING BREAD
Crisp brown skin of pork with all its fat rendered, usually baked into cornbread.

## CRAYFISH (CRAWFISH)
Nickname mudbugs—small edible crustaceans, popular in Creole cooking

## CROQUETTE
Chopped meat crumbled and fried into a crisp brown cylindrical shape. African-Americans usually make Salmon Croquettes served for breakfast.

## ETOUFFEE (A'-TOO-FAY)
Method of cooking during which chicken or shellfish is smothered by chopped vegetables and cooked over a low flame in a tightly closed pan with little or no liquid.  Used in Creole cooking.

## FAT BACK
Fat from the back of a loin of pork, usually salted and used in seasoning greens.  Very popular in African-American cooking.

## FILÉ POWDER
Dried ground sassafras leaves used as a flavoring and a thickening ingredient for gumbo.  Used in Creole cooking.

## FUFU
A starchy substance made from fermented cassavas.  This is an African dish.

## FRIED PIES
Filled with peaches or apples—usually deep fried. They are also called half moon pies, made with a circle of dough folded in half.

## FRITTERS
Food, either savory or sweet, dipped into batter and deep fried.  Popular in Caribbean and African cooking.

## GROUNDNUTS
Peanuts; used in African cooking.

## GUMBO
A thick Creole soup or dish thickened with okra and filé powder.  The word gumbo is derived from an African word for okra.

## HOE CAKES
Bread which slaves baked over open fire in fields on the blade of a hoe.

## HOME FRIES
Sliced or cubed potatoes fried in bacon fat, not mashed like hash brown potatoes.  They retain their shape and are usually eaten at breakfast.

## HOMINY OR GRITS
Coarsely ground hulled cornmeal bleached white and eaten boiled, with butter or gravy, usually eaten for breakfast.  Hominy is of American Indian origin and very popular in the southern states.

## HOPPING JOHN

A dish of rice and peas usually black-eyed peas; a staple of African-American cooking in the south and Caribbean and traditionally served on New Year's Day.

## HUSH PUPPIES

Deep-fried cornmeal dumplings, usually eaten with fried fish. They are popular in the south.

## JAMBALAYA

A dish from Cajun cuisine of rice with ham, shell fish, sausage, chicken, beans and vegetables seasoned with Creole spices.

## LARD

Rendered pork fat, used for deep-frying and flaky pastry.

## MONKEV BREAD

Sometimes called bubble bread, made of separate clumps of dough piled and baked in a tube pan.

## OKRA

Small sticky green pods of the okra plant. Native to Africa and brought to the southern states with the slave trade. It is used as a vegetable and a thickener for soups, stews and gumbos and is very popular in Creole cooking.

## PEANUTS

Not a true nut but the seed of a leguminous bush. Brought to the United States as a result of the slave trade, this highly nutritious food is a staple in Africa. George Washington Carver's experiments produced over 300 ways to use the peanut.

## PECANS

Nuts from the south used in pies and pralines—important dessert nut in the United States. The name is of American Indian origin.

## PLANTAIN

Fruit that looks like a very large banana, known as green banana, sometimes short and fat with a green, deep red or yellow skin. It is usually fried or baked and popular in Caribbean cooking.

## POT LIKKER

The broth remaining after greens and vegetables have been cooked. It is nutritious and an essential part of African-American cooking—usually served with corn bread or corn pones.

## RED BEANS AND RICE

A Louisiana specialty of red beans (sometimes kidney beans) and rice, cooked with ham hocks. There are many variations.

## RED EYE GRAVY

Ham gravy made with ice water or even coffee. Served in the south for breakfast with grits and biscuits.

## RICE

A grain that is very popular along the southern coast and throughout the Caribbean where it has been eaten for more than 300 years. It has become an integral part of African-American cookery, such as, Creole (gumbo), Red Beans and Rice and Hoppin' John in South Carolina.

## ROUX - (roo)

A mixture of flour and butter or other fat, usually in equal proportions, cooked together slowly and used to thicken sauces and soups. Roux means reddish or reddish brown. Very popular in Creole cooking for gumbo.

## SCRATCH CAKE

A cake made from scratch, using a recipe and not a box of cake mix.

## SOP

To use a piece of food as bread and dip it into the sauce. In African-American cooking, biscuits are sopped in molasses.

## SPOON BREAD

Made from cornmeal and eggs. The consistency of spoon bread is more like that of pudding. It is light and soft enough to be served with a spoon.

## SWEET POTATOES

A root vegetable often confused with the yam. Sweet potatoes have a reddish skin. Very important in African-American cooking for making sweet potato pies.

## TEA CAKES

Old fashioned cookies.

## WATERMELON

Originated in West Africa, a very popular melon, usually eaten in the summer by African-Americans.

## YAMS

A tuberous vegetable, has white or yellow flesh and brown skin and is often confused with sweet potatoes. Candied yams is a very popular dish in the African-American home.

# ORDER FORM

## THE AFRICAN-AMERICAN CHILD'S HERITAGE COOKBOOK

**POSTAL ORDERS:** Sandcastle Publishing, Customer Service—Order Dept., P.O. Box 3070, South Pasadena, CA 91031-6070 U.S.A.

**Please send the following books. I understand that I may return any books in unmarked and resalable condition for a full refund—for any reason, no questions asked withing 7 days of receipt of the book.**

Number of Books Ordered: _____

Cost of Books:          $19.95 x _____          = _____

Sales Tax:                              =          _____

Please add $1.65 for books shipped *to* a California address.
(8.25% CA sales tax)

Shipping:                              =          $4.25

TOTAL                              =          _____

Please send my order to:

_____
Name

_____
Address

_____
City                    State                    Zip Code

_____
Daytime Phone Number with area code first

*Thank you*